DORINDA'S
Taste of the
CARIBBEAN

DORINDA'S
Taste of the
CARIBBEAN

AFRICAN-INFLUENCED RECIPES
FROM THE ISLANDS

Dorinda Hafner

TEN SPEED PRESS
Berkeley, California

ACKNOWLEDGMENTS

Thanks to: Clancy Drake, my editor ("…aah, Ms. Drake, you've done it again!"), for holding the safety net; Janine Cesnich, my chef's assistant, typist, and food tester, for the hours and hours of support and the many midnight-to-dawn forays in my kitchen; David Kuchel, Janine's husband and ever-patient guinea pig, for the critical gourmet you are, we're grateful you've given Caribbean food the nod; Janine "JAFFA" Baigent, my kitchen assistant and general "go for!", for all your work—one day we'll convince you to handle meat without fear; Aku Kadogo—remember, sister girl, we will be there; Cath Kerry, the food stylist, and Milton Wordley, the photographer, for the fun; and Sue Sheppherd and Cassie Farrell, my "belle" pair from England, for your faith in me and in the T.V. series "A Taste of the Caribbean."

Many thanks to my U.K. film crew and my Caribbean support team: Maxine Walters; Peter Packer; Dr. Mackenzie; Annette Alfred; Yolande Cools-Latigue; Loye, Aimi, and Bernie Barnard; Tony Poyer; Julian Clinkard; Tom Stevenson; Geoff "Brillo" Quick; the Geezer; Rachel Pinnock; the Cuisinières of Guadeloupe— Mesdames Plocoste, La Cross, Jean Plu Main, Felix, Lousianne, Violet, and Rozanne; Jenny Lindeborg; Sonia Garmers; and Issoco.

A Kirsty Melville book

1🟦
TEN SPEED PRESS
P.O. Box 7123
Berkeley, CA 94707

Distributed in Australia by E.J. Dwyer Pty Ltd; in Canada by Publishers Group West; in New Zealand by Tandem Press; in South Africa by Real Books; and in the United Kingdom and Europe by Airlift Books.

Cover design by Nancy Austin and Catherine Jacobes
Interior design by Sarah Levin and Nadja Lazansky
Illustrations by Diana Reiss
Printed in Hong Kong

Library of Congress Cataloging in Publication Data
Hafner, Dorinda.
Dorinda's taste of the Caribbean/ by Dorinda Hafner.
    p. cm.
Includes index.
ISBN 0-89815-836-2
1. Cookery, West Indian. 2. West Indies—Social life and customs.
I. Title.
TX716.W4H34 1996
641.59729—dc20   96-13920   CIP

1 2 3 4 5—99 98 97 96

FOREWORD

When Dorinda Hafner first burst on our consciousness with her book, *A Taste of Africa,* and the subsequent television series of the same name, she was a woman with a mission. In her own words she wanted, "to elucidate and elevate African cuisine to international status." When I first came into contact with her book, I uttered a heartfelt AMEN, for this was a train on which I already traveled. Her first work included recipes not only from the African continent itself, but also from six places in the western hemisphere where the food has been touched by the African continent. Reading it, I learned that Dorinda is also about connections and continuities, indeed a sister traveler on a culinary voyage.

Now, in *Dorinda's Taste of the Caribbean,* she again packs her pots and pans, her sense of history, and her sense of humor and takes them on the road. This time she travels to the Caribbean with a work detailing the African-influenced culinary traditions of that continent of islands. Here, Ghanaian-born Dorinda's work is crucial and unique for it gives us one of our first glimpses of an African woman's view of the evolution of the region's food. With Dorinda, we can taste the *dokono* of Jamaica and learn of its Ghanaian origins, sample the *kalas* of Curaçao and be reminded of the West African *akara,* and delight in the name and taste of the Cuban okra stew—*quimbombo.*

Dorinda's observations of the food of the Caribbean region and her delight in discovery are contagious. A consummate storyteller, Dorinda illuminates her journey with tales and proverbs. The twinkle in her prose, however, is always backed up by solid recipes and a sense of the past prefiguring the present.

If you don't know Dorinda Hafner, meet her in these pages and learn to laugh with her. If you do, savor her again. She is a part of an unbroken circle of tradition, and her placing the food of the Caribbean into the perspective of African-Atlantic continuities is important for us all. But hey…it's not that heavy. It's about good food, great flavors, good fun, and fine people, and you might just learn something on the way.

Jessica Harris
May 1996

Florida
Keys

The Bahamas

Cuba

Jamaica

ATLANTIC

Dominican Republic

Haiti

Virgin Islands

Puerto Rico

Guadeloupe

Dominica

Martinique

St. Lucia

St. Vincent

Barbados

Grenada

Tobago

Curaçao

Trinidad

Contents

INTRODUCTION

God must be from the Caribbean. No particular island, just the area in general. I came to this conclusion during my second visit to the islands. What other reasons could there be for the sheer beauty of the place? The Caribbean is God's own county—for once even holiday brochures do not do it justice.

The Caribbean has many faces. The one that is driven by the tourist industry and is characterized by stunning waiters and waitresses in pristine uniforms serving chilled fruit cocktails laced with rum, bikini-clad bodies frolicking in the foaming surf, and blue, blue seas fringed with endless white sandy beaches is there for the asking, but it is only part of the story.

It is not hard for those of us who live outside the region to restrict our knowledge purely to what is offered in the holiday brochures or to what we see as backdrops in movies or televised sports matches. We are so used to thinking of the Caribbean as a place where colorful, sculptured locals with big smiles of flashing white teeth live laid-back lives in a garden of Eden that we forget that the individual islands have their own rich histories and identities, and are struggling to make their own marks on the world. I visited many of the hundreds of islands and managed to learn quite a bit.

In the summer of 1995, I went to the Caribbean to film a television series and to see for myself some of the other faces of this region. The image of the Caribbean as one big exotic playground with the same people and cultures holds some parallels with notions of my own Africa, a continent referred to for centuries as "the dark continent" and seen as essentially one big romantic country inhabited by blacks. So, needless to say, I went to the Caribbean open and ready to be educated. I only hope that I did not embarrass myself too badly through my exuberant, childlike curiosity!

Some of the first great surprises for me were in the incredibly varied topography and climates of the islands. The breathtaking coastline of the island of Tobago and the lushness of Dominica contrasted stunningly with the arid vistas of Curaçao. Even Curaçao, the most desertlike of all the islands, has its unique beauty in the surreal effect of the tall, spiky cacti with their red and yellow flowers interspersed with the flat-topped, fernlike *palu di inju* trees, all regally holding their ground amidst gusts of dusty wind.

In many of the islands, an abundance of fruit was everywhere: majestic, laden breadfruit trees; coconut palms and mango trees heavy with clusters of ripening fruits; and orange, lime, lemon, and papaya trees covered with their succulent produce. At ground level, masses of heart-shaped green dasheen leaves sprung up from their delicious roots. My admiration for this bounty, I must admit, was tinged with a little jealousy!

It is unfortunate that when most people visit the Caribbean as tourists they tend to eat mostly what is offered in the hotels, rarely venturing out to explore the fare offered in local haunts to the residents. On my visit, I was most interested to see how the culinary branches sent out from my native West Africa had taken root in these islands. I wanted to see what foreign yet familiar fruits those branches bore.

I was fed all sorts of food and drinks, most of which I have tried to share with you in this book. In Curaçao I developed a liking for soursop milkshakes, cool tamarind drinks, *tutu* (a cornmeal dish of African descent), and *kaas yerna* (a Dutch dish of cheese stuffed with meats); in Jamaica I couldn't keep away from barbecue of any sort, especially when it was served with sweet potatoes and washed down with rum punch; in Guadeloupe I decided I love *matété* (crab risotto), *blaff* (fresh fish soup), and *ti-punch* made with rum!

In looking for the African roots in Caribbean cuisines, I have found that some of the traditional foods have changed tremendously and some have not changed at all. Some of the foods were familiar to me, like the "ground provisions" of plantains, dasheen, sweet potatoes, yams, and cassava. Others looked familiar but had different names, like sky juice (fruit cordial on crushed ice) and *coucou* (cornmeal and okra). Still others had recognizable names but looked different, like *quimbombo,* a Cuban okra stew, or *dokono,* a Jamaican sweet. The latter is actually from my part of the world, Ghana. *Dokono* is an Akan name for savory, fermented cornmeal dough wrapped in banana leaves and steamed; but in Jamaica, this dish is sweet and bears little resemblance to the original. In Dominica, it is called *conky,* a word that sounds like an adulteration of the word *kenkey,* which is the name of southern Ghana's version of *dokono.* This is smaller than the Akan version, and is wrapped in corn husks, not banana leaves. Again, the Dominican version is very different: it is sweet, and is made with cassava, sugar, and spices. Whew!

I also had many totally new experiences, like eating mountain chicken (huge toads), cactus and iguana soup, *bébélé* (roasted breadfruit and vegetable soup), and *buñuelos* (cassava and aniseed pastries). The constant in the development of all the foods I tried seems to be the ingenuity of the cooks. Slaves and their descendants were brilliant at turning the local produce, such as "ground provisions" and even cactus, and tiny amounts of offcuts and cheap meats into culinary success stories.

As always in writing my cookbooks, I found the research to be as exciting as the manifestation of the recipes themselves. Notwithstanding economic hardships, the people on every island received me with warmth and humor, intrigued by the fact that

I had come from our roots in Africa to trace out our shared culinary branches. With this book and the accompanying television series, I wish to share some of that warmth and humor, and in my modest way to expand on people's image of paradise in the Caribbean. Come with me on a different sort of cross-Atlantic journey, a tour that would make many a plantation owner "shut their mouth wide open and clutch pearls" if they were to see things now. Yer, man, the times, they've been a-changin'.

JAMAICAN RIDDLE

Riddle me this, riddle me that: what am I? "Me bendy bendy, me windy windy, me name in a goverment book."

Answer: A road.

A NOTE ON THE CONVERSIONS
OF MEASUREMENTS

The recipes in this book were tested using conventional imperial measurements, and the metric measurements built into every recipe are close-to-exact conversions of those measurements, rather than approximations. If you use metrics in the kitchen, you can also consult the conversion charts on pages 140 and 141.

CUBA

Cuba is the largest of the Caribbean islands—and certainly one of the most beautiful. The countryside is a veritable labyrinth of natural treasures, including the stunning Vinhales Valley region, which looks so prehistoric you almost expect to see dinosaurs bound into view any minute.

Cuba is very much a country of historical contrasts. The Spanish were the first foreigners to leave their mark on the island, and to this day dilapidated yet grand old Spanish mansions abound in the capital city of Havana, reminding one of a bygone period of opulence and decadence. In the middle part of this century, Cuba was a playground for the world's rich and famous, especially from the nearby United States. In 1959, when Fidel Castro overthrew Fulgencio Batista to become the first Communist premier of Cuba, relations with the noncommunist powers—especially the United States—disintegrated rapidly until finally, in 1962, the U.S. enforced a strict trade embargo against Cuba. For almost thirty years, Soviet subsidies buffered Cuba against economic hardship, but now that the U.S.S.R. has broken up (and the embargo is still in place), Cuba has been left in a serious economic crisis. In part, this means that farmers have resorted to older, less mechanized ways of planting and harvesting, and all the people have had to become ever more ingenious in their cooking.

Unlike on most Caribbean islands, the population of Cuba is primarily of Spanish European descent, with just twenty percent of the people being of African descent. I was therefore surprised to find the links with African culture and cuisine still so strong—especially the connection with the culture, religion, and cuisine of the West African republic of Nigeria. Beans and peas, okra, hot chile peppers, plantains, cassava, rice, and pork are common fare in Cuban cooking. And when it comes to desserts, Cubans have successfully married Spanish sweetness to African savory dishes to produce many mouthwatering confections and treats. Let's try some.

Delia's Tamales

Delia, the country cousin of my Cuban friends Juan Carlos and Raimondo Socarras, made it look so easy when she prepared her tamales. It is easy to make the mixture, but I have since discovered that problems can arise when you try and seal them in the corn husks. Now that takes some practice! But once you have made one tamale, you'll find making the rest a piece of cake! The end result makes the effort worthwhile. I have found that it is best to either pick or buy the corn cobs still with their full husks, not trimmed in any way. This gives you a much wider set of leaves to play with. Delia told me that you can also add pork sausage meat, large amounts of very finely chopped bits of your favorite herbs, gherkin pickles, olives, and other favorite, to your tamale mixture. Part of the fun of eating tamales is the guests' anticipation as they peel off the corn husks to discover what's inside. (Pictured opposite page 4.)

6 fresh corn cobs, each with full set of husks
Husks from 8 additional cobs
¼ cup (57 g) butter
¼ cup (59 mL) olive oil
1 large onion, finely chopped
4 to 6 cloves garlic, very finely chopped
1 or 2 large, fresh, ripe chiles (chillies), seeded and finely chopped
1 green bell pepper (capsicum), seeded and finely chopped

Carefully peel the husks off the corn cobs, taking care not to rip them. Wash each whole husk in cold running water. Dry the husks with paper towels or a clean dishtowel. Cut the husks of 3 or 4 of the cobs lengthwise into long, ½-inch (1-cm) strips, for tying the tamales. Set aside.

Wash each corn cob under running water and remove the long, silky hairs. Dry with a clean dishtowel and grate the kernels of corn off each cob using the fine holes of a cheese grater. Place grated corn in a large bowl, cover, and set aside.

To make the tamale filling, melt the butter and heat the oil in a skillet or saucepan over medium heat. Fry the onion, garlic, chiles, and bell pepper until the onion is golden, about 10 minutes. Add the herbs and cook for a further 3 minutes and then add the tomato paste and continue cooking for a further 4 to 5 minutes. Season with salt and pepper, then remove the pan from the heat and pour the onion mixture into the corn mixture. Stir well to combine, then taste and adjust the seasoning as necessary.

To make the tamales, overlap the edges of 2 or 3 corn husks (depending on their size) with the narrower part of the leaves pointing downward, so that they form a tube. Fold the bottom of the tube up to form a cup, leaving the top open for filling.

Finely chopped fresh
   herbs, such as basil,
   oregano, and chives, to
   taste
2 tablespoons (30 mL)
   tomato paste
Salt and freshly ground
   pepper to taste

Now fill the tube with the corn mixture to two-thirds full. Stand the filled tube in a large empty coffee cup while you make a lid for it from new husks. To make the lid, wrap 2 or 3 new husks around the top of the first tube, with the narrow ends up, totally enveloping the filled tube and enclosing the bottom fold of the first tube.

With one hand securing the middle of the join, use your free hand to fold down the top end of the parcel on the same side as the bottom fold. Tie the tamale vertically and horizontally with two strips of husk, securing each tie with a firm knot. If strips are not long enough, tie them together, securing with a knot. Repeat the process using the rest of the husks and filling.

To cook the tamales, bring about 3 quarts (2.8 L) of water to a boil in a large stockpot. Using a long-handled spoon, carefully place the tamales in the boiling water. Return to a boil and cook for about 30 to 40 minutes, uncovered.

To test whether the tamales are cooked, use the long-handled spoon to remove one from the pot. Place it under cold running water to cool slightly, and give the tamale a little squeeze: it should feel firm if it is cooked. If it does not, return it to the pot for further cooking. Repeat the process until you are sure the tamales are cooked.

Finally, remove all the tamales from the water and drain them on paper towels. Allow the tamales to cool down a little and then serve them either as snacks or as an appetizer, according to your choice.

Variation: You may also cook tamales in a microwave. Arrange the tamales in a microwave-safe dish and cook on High for 10 to 15 minutes. Squeeze to test whether they are done, as above.

MAKES APPROXIMATELY 10 TO 12 TAMALES;
SERVES 4 TO 6 AS AN APPETIZER OR A SNACK

Pescado
RAW FISH PICKLED WITH LIME

My dear friend Raimondo Socarras' father-in-law has a reputation in the family as being the best person to make this dish. I never thought that I could enjoy raw fish as much as I did this *pescado,* so I asked for the recipe and here it is—except that I have personalized it by adding some lemon scented thyme. I have called for fish fillets here, but you may wish to purchase the whole fish and reserve the carcass for another use—that is what they do in Cuba. Serve as an appetizer or as a light lunch with a green salad and crusty fresh bread. Remember, the fish must be marinated overnight.

2 pounds (907 g) white-fleshed fish fillets, such as red snapper
A large bunch of lemon-scented thyme
Juice of 6 to 8 limes
Salt and freshly ground pepper to season
¼ cup (59 mL) tomato ketchup
¼ cup (59 mL) mayonnaise

Use a knife to flake off the flesh of the fish from the skin. Make sure all the bones are removed, and put the fish pieces into a bowl. Strip off the thyme leaves and discard the stalks. Sprinkle the lime juice, salt, pepper, and thyme leaves over the fish pieces, and stir well to combine. Cover and refrigerate overnight. The next day, stir in the ketchup and mayonnaise, and season to taste with salt and pepper. Mix well and serve.

SERVES 4 TO 6 AS AN APPETIZER

Opposite: Delia's Tamales (page 2)
Following pages: Ensalada de Frijoles y Huevos (page 8); Quimbombo (page 10)

Malanga Princessita
TARO FRITTERS

Oh, how I remember the bright young face of Jessica Socarras, my six-year-old Cuban friend, who I renamed Princessita. How her eyes sparkled as she chatted away in Spanish to me, trying to explain how easy it is to prepare malanga. And all I could do was stand there smiling sheepishly at this beautiful young girl, because my Spanish was so bad and I could only make out the odd word here and there. But what I lacked in language I more than made up for in enthusiasm! Yes, this dish is easy to make: if a six-year-old can prepare the malanga for her mother to fry, you should be able to do the lot by yourself.

2 large taros
1 clove garlic, finely
   chopped
1 egg
Salt and freshly ground
   pepper
Oil for deep-frying

Peel and wash the taros. Grate them into long, thin strips using the section on a cheese grater with the biggest holes. In a large bowl, mix the taro with the garlic, egg, and salt and pepper to season. Mix well. Leave to stand, covered, for 10 to 15 minutes.

Pour oil for deep-frying into a deep saucepan. Heat the oil until it is hot but not smoking and drop large spoonfuls of the mixture into the hot oil, frying until the fritters are golden brown, about 1 to 2 minutes. Drain on paper towels and serve hot or warm.

MAKES 8 TO 10 FRITTERS; SERVES 4 AS A SIDE DISH

Opposite: Barbara's Buñuelos (page 12)

Sopa de Frijoles
BEAN SOUP

Every time I come across black-eyed peas in the Caribbean, a feeling of contentment and recognition comes over me. Black-eyed peas are de rigueur in Ghana, but you can use any beans you like.

8 ounces (227 g) black-eyed peas (beans) or other dried beans of your choice
6 cups (1.4 L) water
1 teaspoon salt
1/2 cup (118 mL) olive oil
1 onion, thinly sliced
2 cloves garlic
1 red bell pepper (capsicum), seeded and cut into thin slices
1 large potato, peeled and finely diced
1 small bunch chives, finely chopped
3 cups (710 mL) vegetable or chicken stock
Salt and freshly ground pepper to taste

Soak the beans overnight in cold water to cover. The next day, drain and rinse them under cold running water. Transfer the beans to a saucepan, add the water and the teaspoon of salt, and bring to a boil. Simmer, uncovered, over a medium heat until the beans are soft when squeezed, about 25 to 30 minutes. When they are cooked, drain off the bean water. Reserve the beans. Save the bean water for use instead of the stock, or discard it. If the bean water is not too salty, you can use part water and part bean water.

In a heavy-bottomed stockpot, heat the oil and fry the onion, garlic, bell pepper, potato, and half the chives until the vegetables start to brown, about 8 to 10 minutes. Pour off 2 tablespoons (30 mL) of the oil and save it. Add the beans to the pot. Add the stock (or the bean water) and salt and pepper to taste, and stir. Bring to a boil, then lower the heat and simmer gently, uncovered, until the vegetables are soft and the broth is slightly reduced, about 30 minutes.

Divide the mixture into two. Blend half of the mixture and return it to the pot. To serve, reheat the 2 tablespoons of oil in a small saucepan over a very low heat. Ladle the soup into warmed bowls, drizzle over the hot oil, and sprinkle with the rest of the chopped chives. Serve the soup hot.

SERVES 4 TO 6

Cubans love their pork. Some of my Cuban friends add diced, smoked ham hock to this soup to make it more hearty, but I leave that to you. Others heat up some rosemary oil with garlic in it and drizzle the flavored oil onto the soup just before serving.

Hearty Cuban Chicken Soup

In the 1950s, Cuba's heyday, a lot of people lived very well all the time. Today, economic hardship means that many ingredients are not always readily available and when they are, they are expensive. A soup such as this is a real luxury and can only be made for special occasions when families pool together their food resources and produce a feast.

1 small chicken, washed and cut into quarters
1 onion, finely chopped
1 fresh hot chile (chilli), washed, seeded, and finely chopped
2 cloves garlic, finely chopped
8 ounces (227 g) tomatoes, blanched and chopped into chunks
A handful of chopped fresh parsley leaves
8 ounces (227 g) pumpkin, peeled and cubed
1 large yam, taro, or sweet potato, peeled and cubed
Salt for seasoning
1 tablespoon (14 g) cornstarch (cornflour)
1 cup (237 mL) lowfat milk
4 ounces (113 g) soft bread crumbs
1 tablespoon (14 g) butter
4 whole hard-boiled eggs
Salt and freshly ground pepper

Put the chicken quarters, onion, chile, garlic, tomatoes, parsley, pumpkin, and yam into a large saucepan or stockpot with about 2 quarts (1.9 L) of water. Season with salt and bring to a boil. Reduce the heat, cover, and simmer over a low to medium heat until the liquid has been reduced by approximately half and the chicken and vegetables are cooked and tender, about 1 to 1½ hours.

Remove the chicken quarters from the pot. Transfer the remaining mixture to a blender and blend quickly. When the chicken has cooled, remove all the flesh, chop the meat into bite-sized pieces, and set it aside.

Mix together the cornstarch, milk, and bread crumbs. Melt the butter and add it to the milk mixture. Stir this mixture into the blended soup and blend again so that it is smooth. Pour the soup back into the soup pot, add the chicken meat and hard-boiled eggs, and season to taste. Stir gently without crushing the eggs and heat until thickened. Take care that the soup does not stick to the bottom of the pot. Serve the soup hot, making sure each person has an egg.

SERVES 4

Ensalada de Frijoles y Huevos
BEAN AND EGG SALAD

This is a salad that is easily affordable and nutritious. Frijoles or beans are an extremely popular ingredient in Cuban cooking. Serve with fresh crusty bread. (Pictured between pages 4 and 5.)

1 large red (Spanish) onion, finely sliced

1 clove garlic, finely chopped

2 tablespoons (30 mL) extra virgin olive oil

2 tablespoons (30 mL) avocado oil

¼ cup (59 mL) balsamic or red wine vinegar

¼ cup (59 mL) mayonnaise

1 one-pound (454 g) can navy (haricot) beans

1 fourteen-ounce (397 g) can red kidney beans

Salt and freshly ground pepper for seasoning

6 yard-long beans (snake beans)

2 large outer lettuce leaves

2 hard-boiled eggs

Sprigs of parsley, for garnish

In a large salad bowl, mix together the onion, garlic, olive oil, avocado oil, vinegar, mayonnaise, and navy and kidney beans. Season with salt and pepper.

Braid 3 yard-long beans as you would plait hair, and secure the ends of the braid with short wooden toothpicks. Repeat the process with the remaining 3 yard-long beans to get two fully completed plaits. Steam or boil the plaits until they are cooked but still crisp, about 10 to 15 minutes.

Wash and dry the lettuce leaves. Arrange the lettuce so it completely covers the bottom of a large, round, flat bowl. Carefully arrange the bean salad in the middle of the bowl, making sure the lettuce leaves show around the edge. Place the two bean braids in a circle around the outer edge of the bowl, just inside the lettuce.

Using an egg slicer, slice the hard-boiled eggs vertically. Arrange the eggs in a circle just inside the bean braids. You should be able to see the edges of the lettuce, then the bean braids, then the eggs, and then, in the middle of the bowl, the beans!

Sprinkle over salt and pepper to taste, garnish with parsley, and serve.

SERVES 4 TO 6

Puerco Cubano
ROAST PORK CUBAN-STYLE

Cuba has the biggest mangoes I have ever seen in my life. They are like baby watermelons, and I found that slices of ripe mango go brilliantly with the barbecued pork. So feel free to try this with your local mangoes.

1 two-pound (907 g) leg of pork
3 cloves garlic, cut into slivers
Salt and paprika for seasoning
Juice of 2 sour oranges (or use 4 limes)

Preheat the oven to 525°F (275°C).

With a sharp knife, score deep cuts into the leg of pork. Stuff these cuts with the garlic, salt, and paprika. Rub what is left over the outside of the meat and generously pour the citrus juice all over the pork and into the scored cuts.

Roast the pork, covered with aluminum foil, in the oven for 30 minutes, then lower the temperature to 350°F (180°C/gas mark 4) and cook for a further 30 minutes, removing the foil so that the pork can brown. The pork can also be cooked in a Weber grill (barbecue), or, if you have half a day to spare, go the whole hog and cook it the Cuban way—barbecued very slowly over burning aromatic wood, such as mesquite or hickory. You must arrange this process carefully (see sidebar). Cooking the pork the Cuban way will take about 2 hours.

SERVES 4

ROASTING PORK THE CUBAN COUNTRY WAY

Clamp the pork between two barbecue grates. The leg of pork should then be suspended by a very thick rope from the branches of a big tree in the garden so that the grates hang down and are about 1 foot (30 cm) above the wood fire.

Now comes the important bit. Another thick piece of rope should be attached to the front of the grates and then to your wrist or ankle while you sit at a reasonably safe distance of about 3 to 4 feet (1 m) away from the fire. The idea is to have the wood fire burning smack bang under the center of the pork and grates, where smoke and heat will best reach the meat. Your job with the front rope is to pull on it at intervals, keeping the meat gently moving, pendulum fashion, while it slowly cooks. (It is advisable to take an interesting book with you to this task.) It is a truly enjoyable pastime—slowly swinging your dinner over the hot coals in the garden on a sunny afternoon.

Quimbombo

PORK AND OKRA STEW WITH PLANTAIN

A Cuban national favorite, this dish caught me completely by surprise. I knew of many of the African connections in Cuba, but it never occurred to me that there would be a Cuban equivalent of the traditional West African okro (okra) stew—and here it was, complete with the magnificent name of *quimbombo*. I guess the difference here is that, unlike its West African counterparts, it does not include eggplant, tomatoes, seafood, or ginger in the ingredients, but it has a distinctive Cuban stamp with the flattened, semiripe *platanos* (plantains) and pork—and it is equally delicious. The plantain adds color and texture to the *quimbombo*. Serve this stew hot with plain rice, rice and peas, boiled taro or cassava, or by itself. (Pictured between pages 4 and 5.)

2 pounds (907 g) pork loin, all fat removed, and diced
Salt for seasoning
1 fresh habanero or red serrano chile (chilli), seeded and finely diced
4 cloves garlic, finely chopped
¾ cup (177 mL) corn oil, plus extra for deep-frying the plantains
2 large onions, finely chopped
6 fresh ripe tomatoes, blanched, skins removed, and diced
2 cups (473 mL) water or chicken stock
1 pound (454 g) okra, topped and tailed, and sliced into thin rounds
2 semiripe plantains, peeled and cut into ½ inch (1 cm)-thick rounds

Season the pork with the salt, chile, and garlic. Allow to stand for about 30 minutes. Heat the oil in a large, heavy-based saucepan until it is very hot, and fry the seasoned pork until golden, about 7 to 10 minutes. Then add the onions and cook over a medium heat until the pork is browned and the onions are cooked and golden, about another 10 minutes.

Add the tomatoes and half the water. Cook for a further 5 minutes, then add the okra. Stir, season to taste, reduce the heat, and allow to simmer slowly, uncovered.

In a separate saucepan, pour in oil for deep-frying and heat it over a high heat until hot. Drop in the plantain rounds and deep-fry quickly. Remove the rounds with a slotted spoon and drain excess oil on paper towels. Flatten each round in the center to resemble a squashed disk or a flattened wheel.

When the pork has been simmering for about 20 to 35 minutes, add the plantain wheels and the remaining water or stock. Stir in the plantain so that it absorbs some of the juices, but be careful not to squash it. Taste and adjust the seasoning. Continue simmering the mixture over a low heat until the liquid has reduced somewhat and the pork is soft and tender, about 10 to 15 minutes. Stir regularly to prevent the stew from sticking to the pan. Serve hot.

SERVES 4 TO 6

Arroz Negro con Calamares
BLACK RICE WITH CALAMARI

O nly twenty percent of the Cuban population is of African descent, and yet that twenty percent makes a significant contribution to Cuban culture. When a friend gave me this recipe, passed on from his African grandmother, I felt honored. In Cuba, instead of fresh calamari, they use canned calamari in its own black ink. This dish can be accompanied by a salad or vegetables of your choice, and a bottle of dry white wine.

7 ounces (198 g) wild black rice

¼ cup (59 mL) olive oil

1 onion, chopped into fine strips

2 cloves garlic, finely chopped

A handful of fresh thyme leaves

1 cup (237 mL) red wine

2 cups (473 mL) clear fish stock

2 cups (473 mL) coconut milk

Salt and pepper to taste

1 pound (454 g) fresh calamari, cleaned and cut into rings

4 lemon slices, for garnish

2 tablespoons chopped chives, for garnish

Put the wild rice in a bowl and cover it with cold water. Leave it for a few minutes, drain, rinse, and drain again.

Heat the oil in a heavy-based, nonstick saucepan or skillet. Fry the onion, garlic, and thyme for about 4 to 5 minutes, or until the onion is light brown. Add the red wine, half the stock, and half the coconut milk. Bring to a boil.

Add the rice to the pan and season with salt and pepper. Reduce the heat, cover, and allow to simmer for about 1 hour. Stir occasionally to make sure the rice is not sticking to the pan. If the rice has absorbed most of the liquid after the first hour of cooking, add another cup of coconut milk and the remaining stock. Cook for a further 30 minutes.

The calamari should be added to the rice in the last 10 to 15 minutes of cooking time. Do not add it any sooner or the calamari will become tough. Serve hot with a slice of lemon on the side of each serving and a sprinkling of chives on top.

SERVES 4 AS A MAIN DISH

W ild black rice is actually the grains of an aquatic grass native to Canada. Wild rice takes longer to cook than regular rice and when cooked, it doubles in size, while ordinary rice quadruples in size. You can use brown rice for this recipe, with the ink from the calamari to darken it, but I prefer the distinctive texture and ease of use of black rice.

Barbara's Buñuelos
CASSAVA FRITTERS WITH SWEET LIME SYRUP

"¡Que linda eres, Barbara!"— "How pretty you are, Barbara!" That's what I kept saying all the time to Barbara Socarras, Raimondo's wife. She is indeed a dark-haired Spanish beauty with culinary skills to match her looks. What I like about her is that she has not given up trying to get Raimondo to do the cooking and in this regard, she has enlisted the help of her mother. So far so good. Raimondo is in the kitchen and wearing an apron. There is hope, because both of them taught me how to make these delicious buñuelos. Believe it or not, cassava is as widely eaten in my neck of the woods in Ghana as it is in Cuba. Serve hot sprinkled with superfine (caster) sugar and fresh lime or lemon zest. (Pictured opposite page 5.)

1 pound (454 g) cassava
Pinch of salt
1⅛ cups (355 mL) all-purpose (plain) flour, plus extra for kneading and rolling
1 egg, beaten
½ teaspoon crushed aniseed
Oil for deep-frying
Zest of 1 lime, for garnish
Superfine (caster) sugar, for garnish (optional)

It is best to use fresh cassava for this recipe. However, if you live in a part of the world where this is hard to come by, then feel free to use the frozen variety. If using fresh cassava, peel off the outer skin, then top and tail and wash the flesh thoroughly with lots of cold water.

Grate the cassava tubers finely by hand or in a food processor. Place the cassava in a large bowl and fold in the salt, flour, egg, and aniseed. Mix until the dough is combined. Flour a pastry board and start to knead and stretch the mixture on the board until it is no longer sticky. At this stage, it should be firm and malleable, rather like soft bread dough.

Divide the dough equally into 16 to 24 small portions (depending on how thick you want your buñuelos to be) and then roll them into long, thin sausages, about 10 inches (25 cm) long. Fold each sausage into a figure-eight shape and stick the ends together with a dab of water.

In a large, heavy-bottomed saucepan, pour in oil for deep-frying. Heat the oil over a medium heat until hot but not smoking, and deep-fry the buñuelos in small batches until they are golden all over, about 1 to 1½ minutes each. Remove from the oil with a slotted spoon and drain any excess oil on paper towels. Cover and keep hot.

SWEET LIME SYRUP

1 cup (237 mL) water
³/₄ cup plus 2 tablespoons (192 mL) sugar
¹/₄ cup (59 mL) freshly squeezed lime juice (about 2 large limes)

To make the syrup, put the cup of water, the sugar, and the lime juice in a saucepan and bring to a boil, stirring all the time as the sugar fully dissolves. Continue boiling and stirring until the liquid is reduced by half, then remove from heat.

To serve, place fresh hot buñuelos on a serving plate. Pour the syrup over the buñuelos, garnish with lime zest and superfine sugar (if desired), and serve.

MAKES 16 TO 24 BUÑUELOS

If, like me, you are not very fond of aniseed, yet you'd like to maintain the authenticity of this recipe, think laterally and instead of the crushed aniseed, add a teaspoon of the anise-flavored liqueur, sambuca. It will give the recipe a hint of anise flavor, and most of the alcohol will evaporate in the cooking.

Pudín Diplomático Cubano
DIPLOMATIC PUDDING CUBAN-STYLE

Desserts are where the Spanish influence in Cuban cuisine becomes apparent, because it is certainly not very African to eat a dessert after a meal. Africans would usually settle for a main meal, with perhaps a piece of fresh fruit. In this recipe—called "Diplomatic Pudding" for its inclusion of Cuba's Spanish, African, and indigenous influences—one could say that African fruit meets Spanish sweetness.

1 cup (237 mL) milk
1 small cinnamon stick
1 small vanilla bean
1 small piece of lemon zest, about 1 inch (2.5 cm) long
3 eggs
½ cup plus 2 tablespoons (142 g) superfine (caster) sugar
Pinch of salt
2 tablespoons (30 mL) crème de cacao liqueur
2 tablespoons (15 g) confectioners' (icing) sugar
12 ounces (340 g) mixed tropical fruit pieces, such as pineapple, peach, mango, guava, and passion fruit, or canned tropical fruit salad (well drained)
8 lady (sponge biscuit) fingers or 6 slices stale sponge cake, enough to cover the top of the baking dish
Heavy (double) cream, for topping (optional)

Preheat the oven to 350°F (180°C/gas mark 4).

Pour the milk into a saucepan, and add the cinnamon stick, vanilla bean, and lemon zest. Bring to a boil, taking care the milk does not burn, lower the heat and simmer for about 4 to 5 minutes, stirring constantly. Remove from the heat and leave to cool for about 10 minutes before removing the cinnamon stick, vanilla bean, and lemon zest.

In a large bowl, whisk the eggs until they are frothy, then add the superfine sugar, salt, and liqueur. Continue to whisk together until smooth and blended. Pour in the milk mixture and stir until thoroughly mixed.

Grease a 6-inch (15-cm) diameter soufflé dish and, using a sieve, sprinkle over the confectioners' sugar. Pour the mixture into the dish and leave to stand for a further 15 to 20 minutes. Arrange the fruit on top of the mixture.

Using the lady fingers, cover the fruit in an attractive radial pattern, working from the center outward until the whole top is covered.

Bake uncovered in a bain-marie (see page 142) in the oven for about 1½ hours or until well set and golden. Remove the trifle from the oven, and leave to cool for 30 minutes before serving. Invert over a serving plate, slice, and serve with or without heavy cream for pouring, as you like.

SERVES 4

Pudín de Coco
COCONUT PUDDING

Coconut is one of the most popular Cuban foods. It is cheap and readily available, and can be drunk and eaten, as well as worn as an adornment and nutrient for the skin, used as decoration, and made into musical instruments. The versatile coconut is a friend to all Cubans. If you cannot find a fresh coconut, use finely shredded coconut and coconut milk, as directed below. To soften the butter, leave it out of the refrigerator for 24 hours or pop it into the microwave for up to 20 seconds on High before use.

1 coconut, or 4 ounces (113 g) finely shredded, desiccated coconut

Scant 1 cup (225 mL) coconut milk (optional)

1/2 cup (227 g) butter, softened

3/4 cup (184 g) superfine (caster) sugar

4 egg yolks

1/2 teaspoon pure vanilla extract

1 tablespoon (7.5 g) confectioners' (icing) sugar

Heavy (double) cream for topping (optional)

Remove the coconut shell and husk and finely grate the flesh by hand or cut it into small pieces and grate it in a food processor. If you are using shredded coconut, mix it with the coconut milk and leave the mixture to stand for 1 hour before using it.

Preheat the oven to 375°F (190°C/gas mark 5).

Whisk the butter and superfine sugar until creamy. Add the egg yolks one at a time, whisking each one in for about 30 seconds as you do so. Add the grated coconut and vanilla extract and continue to whisk for about 3 minutes.

Grease an 8-inch (20-cm) cake pan with some butter. Sprinkle over the confectioners' sugar, turning the pan until the sugar is evenly distributed.

Pour in the mixture and cook in a bain-marie (see page 142) in the oven for about 1 to 1 1/2 hours, or until the pudding is cooked and feels firm to the touch, especially in the center. Remove from the oven and allow to stand for about 20 minutes before serving.

The top of the pudding should be hard like a cookie and the bottom soft. Serve with heavy cream to pour over, if desired.

SERVES 4

Mojito
RUM PUNCH

I had my first *mojito* in November 1989 at the world-famous La Bodigueta del Medio, but that was nowhere near as memorable as my second one—same place, different time—in August 1995. Somehow time and my memory seem to have conspired to improve the taste, and turn me into a converted *mojito* addict.

1 cup (237 mL) Cuban rum
4 large mint sprigs
2 tablespoons (28 g) sugar
1 lime
Lots of crushed ice

Divide the rum, mint, sugar, and lime juice equally between two glasses. Fill each glass with crushed ice. Press down the contents of each glass with a spoon to crush the mint leaves a little, then stir to mix and serve.

SERVES 2

Saoco
CUBAN "PIÑA COLADA"

While filming in Cuba, I was introduced to another drink that is not a daiquiri but more like Cuba's equivalent of a piña colada without the pineapple juice, a strange drink called *saoco*, I think—I am not sure of the spelling since my Spanish is negligible. I would like you to try it, too.

1½ cups (355 mL) coconut milk
1 cup (237 mL) good white rum
¼ cup (57 g) superfine (caster) sugar
2 tablespoons (30 mL) coconut liqueur (optional)
Crushed ice
Tropical flowers, for garnish (optional)

Put all the ingredients, except the ice, into a cocktail shaker, and give them a healthy shake for about 20 to 30 seconds. Place crushed ice in large, long-stemmed glasses (or preferably, coconut shell cups), and pour over the daiquiri. Garnish with exotic tropical flowers, such as hibiscus or tropical frangipani.

SERVES 2

Two Favorite Daiquiris

There are various stories circulating in Cuba about the origins of the daiquiri. A lot of tourist hotels insist that the daiquiri was first requested by Ernest Hemingway, with one or two going as far as to show you his favorite seat at the bar and his favorite daiquiri combination of rum; the clear, orange-based Triple Sec liqueur; lime; and ice. Other locals insist the daiquiri was originated by Cuban miners. Whatever the truth is, any daiquiri combination can see you asking for seconds and thirds. Here are a couple of my favorites.

TRIPLE SEC AND MANGO DAIQUIRI

1/2 cup (118 mL) good white rum
3 tablespoons (43 g) superfine (caster) sugar
1/4 cup (59 mL) Triple Sec
2 tablespoons (30 mL) fresh lime juice
1/4 cup (59 mL) fresh mango juice
Crushed ice
Mint sprigs, for garnish

The secret to a good daiquiri is to shake it and not stir it. So place all the ingredients except the ice in a cocktail shaker and do a little Cuban rumba dance for about 30 seconds while shaking your daiquiri, to put you in the mood. Place crushed ice in 2 stemmed glasses, pour over the daiquiri, and garnish with mint sprigs.

COCONUT DAIQUIRI

1/2 cup good white rum
3 tablespoons (43 g) superfine (caster) sugar
2 tablespoons (30 mL) fresh lime juice
1/4 cup (59 mL) coconut liqueur
1/4 cup (59 mL) coconut milk
Crushed ice
Cubes of fresh pineapple and coconut, for garnish

Place all ingredients except the ice in a cocktail shaker and shake vigorously for about 30 seconds. Place crushed ice in 2 stemmed glasses, pour over the daiquiri, and garnish with pieces of pineapple and coconut, pierced with fancy cocktail sticks.

EACH RECIPE SERVES 2

Curaçao

Curaçao and the neighboring islands of Aruba and Bonaire comprise the Netherlands Antilles—they are also known as the ABC islands. Curaçao is the commercial center of Dutch activities in the Caribbean. It lies just 25 miles (40 km) off the Venezuelan coast. Curaçao is a fascinating place, which curiously juxtaposes arid desert conditions with modern technology and business.

Willemstad, the capital of Curaçao, looks like a miniature Holland—pretty and clean, with well-built, brightly colored houses and fancy Dutch architecture. The island is small—210 square miles (546 km2) in area—but prosperous, with international banking activity, a major oil refinery, and proximity to some of the region's busiest shipping lanes. It has the biggest desalination plant in the southern hemisphere. Curaçao also produces an interesting beer called Amstel, which is made from desalinated water.

The people are a wonderful mixture—mostly descended from Africans, Spanish, and Dutch; plus a mixture of other Europeans, South Americans, and other West Indian islanders.

Like most Caribbean islands, Curaçao has a sad past. At the height of slavery in the seventeenth century, slave warehouses called asientos were set up on Curaçao. Slaves were shipped in from places like Gorée, off the coast of Senegal in West Africa. Those who survived the horrendous journey were held in these asientos to be cleaned up and graded, and then, like other commodities, sold to the highest bidders from surrounding West Indian islands and Brazil.

However, unlike on many other islands, the slaves who were kept on Curaçao did not have to work in sugarcane fields. Nothing would grow well here apart from cactus, so the slaves were put to work on salt pans and as household servants in the big houses (landhuis) of wealthy Dutch merchants.

Kalas
BLACK-EYED PEA PUFFS

This is yet another one of the recipes brought over from Africa. The interesting thing is that, although corrupted over time and translated into a different language, its present name still bears a striking resemblance to the original West African name of *akara.* Other Caribbean islands refer to the dish as *calas, accras,* or *accra;* this last spelling being the same as the name of the capital city of Ghana, the West African republic where I was born. Remember you have to soak the peas overnight. Serve the *kalas* by themselves or with plain tomato ketchup, Asian sweet chile (chilli) sauce, or any sauce of your choice. (Pictured opposite page 20.)

1½ pounds (680 g) black-eyed peas (beans)
½ cup (118 mL) water
2 teaspoons salt
1 small, fresh hot chile (chilli), seeded and chopped, or more according to your taste
Oil for deep-frying

Place the peas in a bowl. Pour over water to cover and soak for 24 hours.

Rinse the peas under cold running water as you rub them together to peel off the outer skins. Drain in a colander and shake off any excess water.

In a food processor, grind the peas very finely in small batches, as you slowly add the water, salt, and chile. The mixture is ready when it is soft, fluffy, and the consistency of cookie dough.

Pour the oil into a frying pan and heat it over a medium heat. Fry small spoonfuls of the mixture, turning regularly until the kalas are golden brown all over. Serve the kalas hot. Makes approximately 50 puffs

Cornmeal Muffins

The African staple, humble cornmeal, is transformed yet again into this more European sweet delight.

1 egg
1 quart (946 mL) milk
¹/₃ cup (78 mL) light (single) cream
Pinch of salt
2¹/₃ cups (375 g) all-purpose (plain) or whole-wheat flour
1²/₃ cups (283 g) yellow cornmeal
2 teaspoons baking powder
8 ounces (227 g) golden raisins (sultanas)
1 cup (227 g) sugar
¹/₃ cup (78 mL) honey
¹/₄ cup (57 g) butter, melted

Preheat the oven to 375° (190°C/gas mark 5).

In a small bowl, combine the egg, milk, and cream and whisk for about 2 to 3 minutes. Whisk in the salt, and set aside. In a large mixing bowl, sift the flour and combine it with the cornmeal, baking powder, sultanas, sugar, honey, and melted butter. Mix well. Make a well in the center of the flour mixture, and pour in the milk and egg mixture. Stir until well combined.

Grease two 12-cup muffin pans, or use greased individual muffin tins arranged on a nonstick baking sheet. Divide the mixture evenly among the cups and bake on the top rack of the oven for 30 to 35 minutes, or until cooked and golden.

Remove from the oven and wait 5 to 10 minutes before turning the muffins out. Serve straight away—hot!

MAKES 24 MUFFINS

Opposite: Kalas (page 19)
Following pages: Spicy Crabs with Cassava Dumplings (page 114);
Roti with Trinidadian Chicken Curry (page 118)

Beef and Coconut Soup

The salt beef needs to be soaked in water overnight, prior to preparing this dish. Serve this hearty soup with Funchi (page 29) or by itself.

1 pound (454 g) salt beef, cubed

2 bay leaves

1 onion, finely chopped

¼ cup (59 mL) corn oil

8 ounces (227 g) mackerel or snook steaks, cleaned

Salt and freshly ground pepper for seasoning

3 cups (710 mL) coconut milk

1 tablespoon tomato paste

1 green bell pepper (capsicum), washed, seeded, and finely chopped

2 tomatoes, blanched, skinned, and coarsely chopped

1 whole small dried chile (chilli)

Pinch of nutmeg

1½ cups (355 mL) vegetable, fish, or beef stock

⅔ cup (113 g) yellow cornmeal (polenta)

2 cups (473 mL) extra water or stock as required

Soak the salt beef in 2 cups (473 mL) cold water overnight to cut down on the salt content. The next day, rinse the beef under cold running water, then place it in a large saucepan. Add 2 cups water and bring to a boil with the bay leaves and the chopped onion. Cook until the meat is tender, about 25 to 30 minutes. Remove the beef, strain and reserve the water, discarding the bay leaves. Set aside the beef, the cooking water, and any leftover onion.

Heat the oil in a deep frying pan or skillet over a medium heat. Season the fish with salt and pepper and sauté until golden on both sides, about 2 to 3 minutes per side. Remove the fish from the oil and allow to cool. Peel off and discard the skin, remove any fish bones from the flesh, break the fish into chunks, and set aside.

Pour the coconut milk and reserved beef water into a large saucepan or Dutch oven. Add the tomato paste, bell pepper, tomato, chile, and nutmeg, and season with black pepper. Stir the mixture, taking care not to crush the chile. Bring to a boil, then reduce the heat and simmer, covered, for about 5 to 10 minutes, or until the vegetables are soft.

Meanwhile, in a bowl, mix the stock with the cornmeal to form a thick paste. Let it sit for about 10 minutes while the soup is simmering.

Add the beef and the fish chunks to the soup. Simmer, covered, for 2 to 3 minutes. Slowly add the paste to the soup to thicken it. Taste, and adjust the seasoning. Adjust the thickness according to taste by adding more coconut milk, stock, or water. Continue to stir regularly so that the soup does not stick to the bottom of the pan. Partially cover and simmer for a further 10 to 15 minutes. Remove and discard the chile pepper, and serve the soup hot.

SERVES 4

Opposite: Christophenes Farcies (page 55)

Sopito de Giambo

OKRA SOUP

Okra is another of the plants thought to have been brought to the Caribbean from Africa during the slave trade days. It has become very popular in many Caribbean islands, with each evolving its own special name (*giambo, gumbo, okro,* or *quimbombo*) and recipes for this glutinous vegetable. In Curaçao, okra is used in soup, and when the early slaves could not grow it because of the aridness of the Curaçaoan soil, they ingeniously substituted the green skin of the local, wild-growing kadushi cactus, which they cut off and pounded up to resemble mashed okra in look, texture, and taste. It did not compromise the taste of the soup whatsoever. The end result, a highly sought-after soup, is called simply *kadushi.*

This soup is very thick and robust because of the okra. The salt beef and the shrimp need to be soaked overnight. You can substitute another oily-fleshed fish such as mackerel for the snook.

8 ounces (227 g) salt beef, rinsed and cut into cubes

3 ounces (85 g) salted dried shrimp

2 sprigs basil (or a Curaçaoan equivalent called *yerba di hole*)

1 small fresh hot chile (chilli), seeded and chopped

12 ounces (340 g) fresh okra, washed and dried, topped and tailed, and cut into thin rounds

1 pig's tail, cut into 2-inch (5 cm) lengths (optional)

Place the salt beef in a bowl, pour over cold water to cover, and soak the meat overnight. Place the dried shrimp in another bowl and soak it also in cold water overnight.

The next day, rinse both the beef and shrimp thoroughly under cold running water to rid them of any remaining salt. Put the shrimp aside.

Bring about 1 quart (946 mL) of water to a boil, add the beef, and boil about 20 to 30 minutes, uncovered. Taste the beef for saltiness. If it is still salty, discard the water, replace it with fresh water, bring to a boil, and boil the beef again as above. Depending on how salty you like your soup, you may wish to save 2 cups of the beef water and use it as stock for the soup.

In a large soup pot or Dutch oven, put the salt beef in the reserved beef water (if used) together with 4 cups (946 mL) of clear water. If you don't use the beef water, then use about 2 quarts (1.9 L) of clear water. Bring to a boil, add the shrimp, basil, chile, okra, and pig's tail (if used). Simmer, covered, over a medium heat for about 30 minutes or until the meat softens, then add the fish and cook for a further 20 minutes.

8 to 10 ounces (227 to 283 g) steaks of snook, mackerel, or similar fish, cut into pieces
Salt and freshly ground pepper to taste

Remove the fish, shrimp, beef, and pig's tail from the soup. Allow 10 to 15 minutes for the fish to cool, then remove the skin and bones. Hand whisk the soup until well blended, about 2 to 3 minutes. Return the fish, shrimp, beef, and pig's tail to the soup, stir, and adjust the seasoning. Serve hot.

SERVES 4

Kadushi is now almost the national dish of Curaçao, although there are Curaçaoans who would insist on giving equal status to other local dishes like Funchi (page 29), Tutu (page 30), and Kaas Yerna (page 28)—and even iguana soup!

Konkomber and Bean Salad

The variety of cucumber that is referred to as *konkomber* in Curaçao looked more like gherkins, or baby cucumbers, to me. If you cannot get *konkombers*, use gherkins, an English cucumber, or a couple of apple cucumbers. The dried peas and beans must be soaked overnight. (Pictured between pages 68 and 69.)

SALAD
8 ounces (227 g) soybeans

2 ounces (57 g) fresh green yard-long (snake) beans

4 ounces (113 g) whole konkombers, or 1 English cucumber, or 2 apple cucumbers

2 ounces (57 g) snow peas (mangetout), topped and tailed

DRESSING
½ cup (118 mL) light olive oil

3 fresh chives, washed and finely chopped

3 sprigs lemon-scented thyme (leaves only)

2 cloves garlic, minced

2 tablespoons (30 mL) lime or lemon juice

2 tablespoons (30 mL) balsamic or wine vinegar

Salt and freshly ground pepper, for seasoning

Soak the soybeans overnight. The next day, place them in a pot with water to cover, bring to a boil, and cook, uncovered, for about 45 minutes or until tender. Drain, and set aside to cool.

Break the yard-long beans into 1-inch (2.5 cm) lengths, and set aside.

Using a fork, score deep grooves down the full length of each cucumber, all the way around its circumference.

Place each cucumber on a chopping board and carefully slice it into fine, thin rounds. When finished, the scoring should make the cucumber slices look pretty and serrated round the edges. Mix the cucumber slices together with the beans and peas in a large salad bowl, and set aside while you make the dressing.

To make the dressing, put the olive oil, chives, thyme leaves, garlic, lime juice, vinegar, salt, and pepper in a jar, cover tightly, hold firmly, and shake well for a few seconds. Pour over the salad and stir thoroughly to mix. Let the salad stand for at least 3 hours before serving.

SERVES 4 TO 6

Salad Greens with Lime Dressing

Curaçaoans generally tend to eat salads with roasts, bakes, grills, or barbecues of fish, meat, and chicken, as opposed to when they eat their more traditional dishes like Funchi (page 29) and Tutu (page 30), which are followed by fresh fruit in the true African tradition. For this recipe, I suggest you use combinations of different colored greens for best aesthetic effect, such as red- and green-leaf lettuce, or radicchio and butter lettuce. (Pictured between pages 68 and 69.)

DRESSING

A very large handful of chopped fresh basil

A handful of fresh lemon-scented thyme leaves or other thyme leaves

¼ cup (59 mL) freshly squeezed lime juice

2 tablespoons (30 mL) avocado oil or extra virgin olive oil

1 teaspoon superfine (caster) sugar

Salt and freshly ground pepper

SALAD

2 lettuces or bunches of salad greens

1 bunch or punnet of sunflower shoots

A handful each of alfalfa shoots and 2 other green salad shoots

6 to 8 ounces (170 to 227 g) snow peas (mangetout), washed, topped, and tailed

1 large avocado

1 whole lime, quartered

1 teaspoon sugar

To make the dressing, combine the basil, thyme, lime juice, avocado oil, superfine sugar, salt, and lots of the pepper in a large jar. Screw down the lid tightly and shake vigorously for about 1 or 2 minutes to mix the contents.

Separate the salad leaves and wash thoroughly. Tear up the leaves coarsely by hand and place in a large salad bowl. Separate the sunflower shoots, alfalfa shoots, and salad shoots by hand and mix them and the snow peas in with the lettuce. Pour the lime vinaigrette over the greens and toss together to mix.

Cut the avocado in half, remove the stone, and douse with the juice from the quartered lime. Slice the avocado, sprinkle it with the 1 teaspoon sugar, and add it to the salad. Toss and serve.

SERVES 4

Papaya Stobá
PAPAYA STEW

In Africa, green papaya is used in place of eggplant (aubergine) when the latter is not in season. Papaya is also used as a meat tenderizer. So it was gratifying to me to see Jenny Lindeborg, my Curaçaoan friend, using green papaya in much the same way in her cooking.

1 pound (454 g) salt beef, cubed
⅓ cup (78 mL) corn oil
1 salted, boiled pig's tail, cut into pieces (optional)
2 onions, finely chopped
3 cloves garlic, finely chopped
1 green bell pepper (capsicum), seeded and finely chopped
2 tomatoes, finely chopped
2 potatoes, peeled and diced
3 pounds (1.4 kg) green papaya, peeled and cubed
Freshly ground pepper

Soak the salt beef in about 2 cups (473 mL) of cold water overnight to cut down on the salt content. The next day, rinse the beef thoroughly under cold water.

Heat the oil in a large saucepan over a medium heat and fry together the pig's tail (if using), beef, onion, garlic, and bell pepper until the onions are transparent and the meat is sealed, about 5 to 10 minutes. Add the tomatoes, potatoes, and papaya. Add pepper to taste, cover, and simmer over a low heat until the potatoes and papaya are cooked and soft and the meat is tender, about 25 to 30 minutes.

The vegetables and meat in this dish release their own juices, preventing the need to add water during the cooking. The green papaya is a natural protein tenderizer and it speeds up the softening of the beef.

SERVES 4

My friend Jenny Lindeborg tells me that when she was growing up in Curaçao, one of their fun traditions was for a single woman looking for a man to discreetly place a sprig of fresh basil behind her ear to make her intentions obvious to prospective interested parties. Basil was not favored just for cooking!

Kabrito Stobá

GOAT STEW

U ntil recently, goat meat has been considered the poor man's food. Increasingly now it is being recognized on many a fancy table as a brother to game. It is often difficult to find goat meat without going to a specialist butcher. If you live in a place where goat meat is not available, I suggest you substitute mutton. This stew should be served hot with rice and cooked vegetables of your choice.

2 beef or vegetable stock
  cubes
1/3 cup (78 mL) corn oil
2 goat's kidneys and 1
  goat's liver, chopped
  (optional)
2 pounds (907 g) goat's
  meat, cleaned and cut
  into bite-sized chunks
2 large onions, finely
  chopped
3 cloves garlic, finely
  chopped
1 small fresh hot chile
  (chilli), seeded and
  finely chopped
1 stick of celery, cleaned
  and finely chopped
8 ounces (227 g) young
  celery leaves, coarsely
  chopped
1 green bell pepper
  (capsicum), seeded and
  thinly sliced
1 ounce (28 g) tomato
  paste
4 small potatoes, peeled
  and left whole
Salt and freshly ground
  pepper to taste

Dissolve the stock cubes in about 1 quart (946 mL) warm water, and set aside.

Heat the oil in a large saucepan. Fry together the goat offal (if used), goat meat, onion, garlic, and chile, until the meat is lightly browned and sealed, about 10 to 15 minutes. Add the celery, celery leaves, bell pepper, tomato paste, potatoes, and stock. Check the seasoning, cover, and simmer over a low to medium heat until the meat is soft and the potatoes are cooked, about 40 minutes to 1 hour. Serve hot with rice and vegetables.

SERVES 4

Kaas Yerna
EDAM CHEESE STUFFED WITH CHICKEN

Of all the dishes that I ate and learned to cook in Curaçao, *kaas yerna* would have to be the one that confirmed Curaçao as Dutch for me—perhaps because of its extravagant use of Edam cheese. *Kaas yerna* is a dish meant to impress, and it lends itself well to culinary experimentation: instead of chicken, you may use lean ground beef or veal, or seafood, or a combination.

4 or 5 boned chicken thighs, meat diced
2 teaspoons paprika
1 teaspoon garlic salt
Freshly ground black pepper
1 whole Edam cheese, about 4 pounds (1.8 kg)
2 tablespoons (28 g) butter
2 tablespoons (30 mL) olive oil
1 onion, finely chopped
1 green bell pepper (capsicum), seeded and finely chopped
1 large tomato, blanched and coarsely chopped
2 tablespoons tomato paste, mixed with a small amount of water
2 tablespoons finely chopped green olives
2 tablespoons peeled, chopped ripe apricot
2 tablespoons (30 mL) curaçao liqueur
2 tablespoons (30 mL) white wine
Salt to taste

Preheat the oven to a 350°F (180°C/gas mark 4).

Season the chicken with paprika, garlic salt, and 1 teaspoon pepper. Toss to coat the meat well. Cover and set aside for about 1 hour.

To prepare your cheese case, cut out about a 1½- to 2-inch (3- to 5-cm) diameter piece from the top of the cheese. Save this to use for the lid later. Leave the outside red wax on to start with while you hollow out the inside of the cheese.

Carefully gouge out the inside from the Edam cheese to make a case, making sure you leave behind a thickness of about ½ inch (1 cm) all round. Save the cheese peices for another use. Carefully remove the red wax from the outside of the cheese.

To make the filling, melt the butter and heat the oil in a skillet or frying pan. Fry the onion, bell pepper, and seasoned chicken together until cooked or until the chicken pieces turn golden brown and the vegetables are cooked, about 15 to 20 minutes.

Add the tomato, tomato paste, olives, apricots, curaçao, and white wine. Stir, season with salt and pepper to taste, and allow to simmer, covered, over a low heat for a further 10 to 15 minutes, stirring regularly.

Fill the cheese case with the mixture and cover with the cheese lid. Bake in the oven for about 15 to 20 minutes, or until the cheese melts and flattens to the touch. Gently transfer it to a serving platter, cut it into four wedges, and serve hot.

SERVES 4

Funchi
CORNMEAL DUMPLINGS CURAÇAO-STYLE

The Curaçaoan version of the ubiquitous cornmeal dumpling is called *funchi*. Interestingly, *funchi* is stirred during cooking with a typically southern African wooden *mealie* or *funchi* stick, while Tutu (page 30) is traditionally whipped with a *lélé*, a kind of tribal food processor. *Funchi* can be served hot or cold with melted cheese on top, or cheese can be stirred in while the *funchi* is cooking. Once it is cold and sliced, it makes a good cold snack for children and adults alike. *Funchi* can be served with salad greens of your choice for a light meal, or it can accompany stews, roasts, and grilled meats.

2 cups (473 mL) water
1 teaspoon salt
1 tablespoon (14 g) butter
2 cups (340 g) cornmeal

In a large saucepan, bring the water to a boil and add the salt and butter. Stir until the butter has melted. Slowly pour in the cornmeal, stirring all the time with a funchi stick or a wooden spoon until the mixture becomes stiff. Remove from the heat, turn the funchi out into a greased dish, allow to cool a little, then form into small balls or shapes as you wish. Serve hot or cold as desired.

SERVES 4 TO 6 AS A SIDE DISH

THE FLOATING PRODUCE MARKETS OF CURAÇAO

The soil of Curaçao is not as fertile as that of other Caribbean islands, so a lot of produce is brought in three times a week from nearby Venezuela to be sold at the floating markets. To visit one of these floating markets is quite an experience—they are a mass of plain and exotic produce arranged for effect on the shelves of makeshift, wooden shopfronts. They are supplied by individual boats moored behind the shops and leisurely bobbing up and down in the sea. It is a spectacle of color and noise, with many voices effortlessly switching languages from the local Papiamento to Spanish to Dutch to English, as bargains are negotiated and acquaintances renewed. And exhausted boat owners nod off to sleep after their journey from Venezuela. The produce boats become their homes while they stay in Curaçao.

Tutu

SAVORY BLACK-EYED PEA AND CORNMEAL CAKES

This dish is yet another Curaçaoan favorite with a direct link to Africa through the island's slave history; to this day, cornmeal is very much a staple of African cuisine. Like a lot of Caribbean dishes of African origin, *tutu* has been given a distinctive Caribbean touch—in this case by adding melted cheese, butter, sugar, and coconut milk instead of using just plain salt and water. The black-eyed peas must be soaked overnight.

8 ounces (227 g) dried black-eyed peas (beans)
1 clove garlic, finely chopped
1 teaspoon salt
2 cups (473 mL) coconut milk
1¹/₃ cup (227 g) cornmeal
¹/₂ cup (128 g) packed brown sugar
4 teaspoons (20 g) butter

CHEESE TOPPING
2 tablespoons (28 g) grated mild cheese
1 tablespoon (14 g) butter

Soak the black-eyed peas overnight in cold water. The next day, rinse them in a colander under cold running water.

Preheat the oven to 375°F (190°C/gas mark 5).

Put the peas, garlic, and salt in a saucepan with 1 quart (946 mL) of water and bring to a boil. Lower the heat and cook, uncovered, until the peas are soft, about 1 to 1¹/₂ hours. Drain.

In a saucepan, warm the coconut milk and then pour it into a food processor (or whip it in a bowl with a traditional lélé), together with the cooked peas and garlic. Add the cornmeal, sugar, and 4 teaspoons butter. Mix together until the mixture is smooth and thick. Transfer the mixture to a medium-sized, buttered casserole dish.

Place the cheese and 1 tablespoon butter in a small saucepan and warm gently over low heat until melted together. Stir this topping and pour it over the tutu. Bake in oven for 10 to 15 minutes, or until golden brown. Let cool very slightly, cut into wedges and serve hot.

SERVES 4

A lélé is a six-pronged wooden agitator, originally from Africa and now found in many Caribbean island kitchens. It has different names according to which island it is found on. It is used like a whisk or egg beater for mashing potatoes or blending soups and so on. *Lélés* come in different sizes—small, medium, and large—and the beauty of a *lélé* is that it is an ecologically sound kitchen implement!

Mint and Mango Ice Cream

Few ice creams have grabbed me the way this one did. It confuses your taste buds totally, causing you to repeat the exercise and eat more!

2 large, or 3 medium, very ripe mangoes

2 sprigs mint, plus extra sprigs for garnish

2 tablespoons (30 mL) mango liqueur, plus extra for garnish (optional)

2 egg whites

¼ cup (57 g) superfine sugar

1¼ cups (296 mL) heavy (double) cream

Wash and peel the mangoes, then cut off all the flesh and put it into a blender together with the mint sprigs. Blend to a pulp, then pour the mixture through a strainer. Add the mango liqueur to the purée. Set aside.

Beat the egg whites together until soft peaks form. In a separate bowl, beat the sugar and cream together until soft peaks form. Fold the mango purée into the egg whites, then fold this mixture into the cream mixture. Pour into an ice cream maker and freeze according to the manufacturer's instructions until firm. Or you may pour the cream mixture into a freezer-safe container or bowl, cover, and leave in the freezer for abut 24 hours, or until firm. If you are not using an ice cream maker, remember to stir the ice cream every few hours or so as it freezes, to stop it becoming icy instead of creamy.

Serve scoops of ice cream garnished with sprigs of mint and, as an added touch, spoon a teaspoon of mango liqueur over each serving if desired.

SERVES 4 TO 6

Skewered Fruits Baked with Curaçao

This is a pretty and easy way to use local fruits and local booze—though on Curaçao, of course, even the "local" fruit is imported! (Pictured opposite page 52.)

2 oranges, peeled and segmented

1 ripe, firm papaya, peeled, seeded, and cut into bite-sized cubes

12 ounces (340 g) watermelon, peeled, seeded, and cut into bite-sized pieces

12 ounces (340 g) pineapple, peeled and cut into bite-sized pieces

2 large, ripe guavas, peeled and cut in half

2 bananas, peeled and cut into 1-inch (2.5 cm) lengths

3/4 cup (85 g) confectioners' (icing) sugar

Juice of 2 lemons

1/2 cup (118 mL) orange curaçao liqueur

Zest of 3 lemons

1/3 cup (78 mL) Grand Marnier

Thread alternate fruit pieces onto each of 4 long metal skewers, making sure to thread the bananas horizontally for the best effect.

In a bowl, combine half the sugar with the lemon juice. Arrange the skewered fruits in a long, narrow dish and pour over the lemon and sugar mixture to marinate for approximately 1 hour, turning skewers at intervals so that all sides of the fruit rest in the marinade.

Preheat the oven to 350°F (180°C/gas mark 4).

Pour off the lemon marinade and combine it with the curaçao, lemon zest, and the remaining sugar in a small saucepan. Stir and heat through over a low heat until the liquid is reduced by half. Remove from the heat, cool, and add the Grand Marnier. Refrigerate to further cool the mixture.

Butter or grease a small baking sheet and arrange the skewered fruit on it. Bake, uncovered, for about 3 to 5 minutes, or until the fruit is heated through. Carefully place the fruit skewers on individual serving dishes. Spoon over the cool syrup and serve.

Variation: You can grill or barbecue the skewered fruits instead of baking them.

SERVES 4

Cesillo
CRÈME CARAMEL CURAÇAO-STYLE

Speed is of the essence when making the caramel for this dish so that the melted sugar does not set too quickly. It is advisable to make the custard first before making the caramel. **Caution:** Hot melted sugar can burn you very badly. Take care when making this mixture.

CUSTARD
4 eggs, separated
1/2 cup (113 g) sugar
2 cups (473 mL) milk
1 vanilla bean or 2 drops vanilla extract

CARAMEL
1 cup (227 g) superfine (caster) sugar
Juice and zest of 1 lime
Pinch of nutmeg

Preheat the oven to 350°F (180°C/gas mark 4).

To make the custard, whip the egg yolks with the sugar until thick and lemon-colored. In a saucepan, heat the milk with the vanilla bean or extract, stirring so the milk does not scald. When the milk is hot but not boiling, remove the saucepan from the heat. Take out the vanilla bean (if using) and stir in the egg yolk mixture. Grease 4 small, individual ramekins or soufflé dishes with butter and set aside while you make the caramel.

To make the caramel, combine the superfine sugar, lime juice and zest, and nutmeg in a small, heavy-bottomed saucepan over a medium heat, stirring until the sugar melts and turns to liquid. Continue to stir until the sugar starts to brown or caramelize. When the sugar turns golden, turn off the heat and use the caramel immediately as follows.

Spoon the caramel mixture into the base of each ramekin. Tilt the ramekins and turn them round so that the caramel coats the sides as well as the bottom. Carefully fill each ramekin with the custard to just under the rim; do not overfill. Cover ramekins with aluminum foil.

Place ramekins in a bain-marie (see page 142) and bake in the oven until firm to the touch or until the custard is set, about 35 to 45 minutes.

Remove, allow to cool down, and chill in the refrigerator until ready to serve. Serve cold.

SERVES 4

Blue Lagoon
CURAÇAO PUNCH

There are many varieties of curaçao liqueur on the market, but I visited Landhuis Chobolobo in Saliña, on the outskirts of Willemstad, where the authentic variety is made. The Landhuis belongs to the Senior family, who manufacture the liqueur. I discovered that apart from the famous blue curaçao, the liqueur comes in four other colors used for making cocktails—red, orange, green, and clear—all of which taste the same. But now different-tasting curaçao is also being produced: coffee, chocolate, and rum raisin. I sampled them all and decided to make this punch in honor of my visit. Triple Sec is an orange-flavored liqueur. (Pictured opposite page 53.)

2 cups (473 mL) blue
    curaçao liqueur
2 cups (473 mL)
    lemonade
2 cups (473 mL) soda
    water
1 cup (237 mL) Triple Sec
½ cup (118 mL) clear
    curaçao liqueur
½ cup (118 mL) clear rum
Assorted sliced fruit, for
    garnish
Lots of crushed ice

Mix all ingredients except the fruit and ice in a punch bowl, stir well, and chill. Add the fruit to the punch when ready to serve, and serve punch in glasses over crushed ice.

MAKES 2 QUARTS (1.9 L)

The Spanish, the first Europeans to arrive on Curaçao (in 1499), had planned to turn it into an agricultural success story by planting sugarcane and Valencia oranges, but the arid soil could not be improved. After years of trying, they gave up. When the Dutch won the island from the Spanish in 1634, they found that they could turn disaster to advantage by using the aromatic oil from the skins of the bitter, shriveled, but now wild-growing Valencia oranges (now referred to locally as Laraha oranges) into a pleasant alcoholic beverage. And so a new drink was born—the blue-colored liqueur called curaçao, which is now probably better known around the world than is its island home. Just how the drink is made, and what gives it its distinctive blue color, remains a secret.

Tamarind Coolers

The tamarind tree has turned out to be quite a bonus in the Caribbean. The tree was initially planted as a windbreak, but the fruits and pods have turned out to be useful too. The ripe pod has a tart, black interior pulp surrounding several seeds. When sugar is added, the pulp can be used to make drinks—on my trips through the Caribbean, I became quite addicted to cold tamarind coolers—and sweet tamarind balls, a very popular dessert sold in markets. In its tart state, tamarind pulp can be used to season fish or meat dishes, curries, and stews. Tamarind also plays an important role in the making of angostura bitters, the famous Trinidadian export, whose recipe must forever remain a secret. Concentrated tamarind paste can be bought in jars or blocks in most Caribbean or Asian specialty stores. This cooler is slightly tart, and it looks like frothy stout beer—it's delicious!

2 tablespoons concentrated tamarind paste
½ cup (113 g) superfine (caster) sugar, or more to taste
1 quart (946 mL) ice cold water, mineral water, or soda water
Crushed ice

Pour half the chilled water into a blender. Add the sugar and the thick but runny tamarind paste and blend on high speed for approximately 20 seconds or until everything is well blended. (It goes slightly frothy, which is why you need to blend only half the water with the tamarind.) Pour into a big jug and add the remaining water and crushed ice. Add more sugar and stir to dissolve if you prefer a very sweet taste. Serve cold in tall glasses.

MAKES 1 QUART (946 ML)

Tamarind fruit is dark and slightly tangy tasting. The pulp is used in various recipes from curries to savory stews and sauces, and with sugar it is added to candy and drinks. Tamarind trees grow freely throughout the Caribbean. They grow tall, up to about 50 feet (15 m), and were originally brought here from the Eastern Hemisphere to grow for windbreaks. Everyone who has eaten Worcestershire sauce has tasted tamarind, as it is one of the sauce's main ingredients.

DOMINICA

Dominica, a member of the British Commonwealth, is a tiny volcanic island only 29 miles long by 16 miles wide (46 by 25 km), flanked to the north and south by the much larger French islands of Guadeloupe and Martinique. What this little island lacks in size, it more than makes up for in defiant beauty.

The original Amerindian inhabitants named Dominica *Waitukubuli,* or "tall is her body." The island is a nature lover's paradise that refuses to be tamed. A ruggedly beautiful mountainous terrain is cloaked in the secrecy of mist, with lush green vegetation, stunning waterfalls, fresh tumbling streams, and many species of intensely colored flora and fauna. There is so much fresh water on Dominica that the nation actually exports it to surrounding islands.

Lennox Honychurch, writing about the island's cuisine in *Dominica: Isle of Adventure,* said:

> Dominica's traditional cuisine, like its history, folklore, and language, is a reflection of Creole mixture and adaptation since the eighteenth century. The mixture is French, West African, and Carib. The adaptation of ingredients was made from what the land provided and what could be conjured up from the staple plantation rations of two hundred years ago… By adding fish and game from the sea and forest, fruit and vegetables from the field, with a liberal variety of herbs and spices, miracles were conjured up.

Dominica's soil is its larder: all you could want to eat is right there for the taking. As Honychurch suggests, the inhabitants of the island learned to be creative cooks. One unusual ingredient, the toad used in the national dish *crapaud,* or "mountain chicken," is caught by moonlight!

The recipes I have taken from this island make good use of the abundant bananas and plantains, coconuts, and citrus fruits of Dominica. As elsewhere in the Caribbean, found the strong influence of African cooking here, in dishes such as Anansis or "Plantain Spiders" (page 37) and "Ground Provisions" and Shrimp Au Gratin (page 46)—all made deliciously exotic with the use of native ingredients and a touch of Europe.

Opposite: Chicken Sankotch (page 45)

Anansis
PLANTAIN SPIDERS

It is entirely suitable that a dish named after Anansi, the spider hero of many local and African traditional tales, should be served somewhere in the Caribbean. The fact that the dish is made out of plantains or bananas is even more fitting, both because there are so many Dominicans of West African descent and because bananas are Dominica's chief crop. This particular dish also goes by the exotic name of *T'zag D'ea.*

I first had *anansis* at Petit Coulibri, an ecotourist haven nestled in the mountains of Soufrière, run by my friends Barni and Loye Barnard. I behaved like a little girl who had discovered a long lost toy; my Grandma used to make plantain and taro *anansis* for us kids when we were growing up in Ghana, and here they were cherished in Dominica. The African connections live on…. (Pictured opposite.)

3 large green or semiripe plantains
Salt to taste
Vegetable oil for deep frying
Flowers, for garnish

Trim off the top and tail of each plantain. Cut the plantains in half and peel off the skin by hand. Coarsely grate the flesh, using the large holes of a cheese grater. Sprinkle with salt and mix well. Allow to stand for about 10 minutes

Heat the oil for deep frying in a heavy-bottomed saucepan. Fry spoonfuls of plantain until crisp and golden, about 1 or 2 minutes. Remove from the oil, drain on paper towels, and serve hot or cold, garnished with tropical flowers.

Variation: Squeeze the juice of 1 lime and mix it with a heaped tablespoon of sugar and a pinch of nutmeg. Add the mixture to the grated plantain instead of the salt and fry as above. This version works well with firm, semiripe plantains.

MAKES APPROXIMATELY 12 ANANSIS;
SERVES 4 TO 6 AS AN APPETIZER OR SIDE DISH

If you are not used to peeling plantain, here's a little tip. Rub your hands very lightly with a little oil or with half a lime before you peel off the skin. This will stop your hands from going black—plantain skin has a habit of leaving dark marks on nails and fingers.

Banana Bread

Banana bread is common to all the Caribbean islands; my Dominican friends say that small, sweet, sun-ripened bananas are the best for this recipe.

½ cup (118 mL) milk
1 vanilla bean or 1 teaspoon vanilla extract
½ cup (113 g) butter
1 cup (255 g) packed dark brown sugar
1 egg
3 or 4 very overripe bananas, peeled and mashed to a smooth consistency
2 cups (340 g) all-purpose (plain) flour
1 tablespoon baking powder
Pinch of salt
½ teaspoon freshly grated nutmeg
Zest of 1 lime

Preheat oven to 350°F (180°C/gas mark 4).

In a saucepan over a low heat, warm the milk and add the vanilla bean. The milk must only be lukewarm to absorb the vanilla flavor. Remove the pan from the heat and leave it to stand until needed.

Cream the butter and sugar together until light and pale. Add the egg, beat for 1 minute, then gradually add the bananas, beating all the time.

Sift the flour, baking powder, salt, and nutmeg together. Fold into the banana mixture and add the zest of lime. Remove the vanilla bean from the milk and add the milk to the mixture. Stir mixture until it is firm but not stiff.

Grease a large loaf pan and pour the mixture into it. Bake in the oven for about 1 hour, or until a skewer inserted in the center comes out clean.

Variation: You may add ¼ cup (59 mL) banana liqueur to the mixture when you add the milk.

SERVES 4 TO 6

Fried Ripe Plantains

A word of warning: this simple dish is addictive! It works so well as an appetizer, snack, or dessert that one can easily develop a craving for it. It is loved by young and old alike. Fried, ripe plantain is simply delicious. Roast some peanuts (groundnuts) for an irresistable combination with this dish.

4 ripe, firm plantains
Salt and freshly ground
    pepper to taste
Oil for deep-frying

Peel off the skins of the plantains. Cut each plantain into thirds horizontally. Then stand each section up and cut into half vertically. With a small knife, score down either side of the central column of seeds and remove the long dark strip of seeds.

Sprinkle salt and pepper over the plantain sections. Pour oil for deep-frying into a saucepan and heat until very hot but not smoking. Quickly deep-fry the plantains in the oil until golden, about 30 to 45 seconds. Remove from the oil, drain on absorbent paper towels, and serve hot.

Variation: For a sweet alternative, fry the plantains without the salt and pepper. Instead, mix together $\frac{1}{2}$ cup (57 g) of confectioners' (icing) sugar, $\frac{1}{2}$ teaspoon of ground nutmeg, and $\frac{1}{4}$ teaspoon of allspice, and sprinkle this all over the fried plantains. Serve hot with ice cream or heavy (double) cream.

SERVES 4 AS AN APPETIZER OR SIDE DISH

Plantain Fried Rice

Sometimes less is more, as this dish proves. It can be eaten plain or as an accompaniment to another dish. (Pictured between pages 68 and 69.)

4 firm, ripe plantains, fried as in preceding recipe
3 cups (500 g) hot, cooked long-grain rice or brown rice
1 sprig parsley, for garnish

Divide the fried plantains into two portions. Save one portion for the garnish, and cut up the other portion into tiny pieces. Mix the plantain pieces in with the hot rice and place in a serving dish. Garnish with remaining fried plantains and parsley. Serve hot.

SERVES 4 AS A SIDE DISH

Plantain Soup

If you are beginning to think Dominicans love their plantains and bananas, you are right! Bananas are the country's main export and the locals can cook myriad recipes with the humble banana. It reminds me of the Chagga tribe at the base of Mt. Kilimanjaro in Tanzania; they are called the banana people.

3 green or semiripe plantains
1 quart (946 mL) beef, fish, vegetable or chicken stock
2 cups (473 mL) coconut milk
Salt and freshly ground pepper to taste
1 chile (chilli), such as Scotch bonnet or habanero
1 bunch cilantro (fresh coriander), leaves only, chopped, for garnish

Peel the plantains and cut them into thick rounds. In a large saucepan, combine the plantain, stock, and coconut milk. Season with salt and pepper and bring to a boil. Add the chile and cook over medium heat until the plantains are soft, about 15 to 20 minutes.

Remove the saucepan from the heat and allow the mixture to cool. Discard the hot pepper and transfer the remaining soup to a blender. Blend until thick and smooth. Return to the saucepan to warm through before serving. Serve hot, garnished with cilantro.

SERVES 4 AS A SIDE DISH

Dasheen, Spinach, and Sweet Corn Soup

Dasheen is another name for taro. Instead of taro (also known as cocoyam or eddoe), you can substitute yams.

2 cobs fresh corn

1 onion, finely chopped

2 cloves garlic, finely chopped

1 pound (454 g) taro or dasheen, peeled and cut into thick cubes

2 tomatoes

6 cups (1.4 L) vegetable or chicken stock

1 cup (237 mL) coconut milk

Salt for seasoning

1 small, fresh hot chile (chilli)

Half a small bunch of spinach or Swiss chard (silverbeet)

Remove the husks and silky hair from the corncobs, clean them, and cut the cobs into ½-inch (1-cm) thick rounds. In a stockpot or large saucepan, combine the onion, garlic, corn, taro, tomatoes, stock, coconut milk, salt, and chile. Bring the mixture to a boil over a high heat. Lower the heat and simmer gently, partly covered, until the corn is soft and cooked and the root vegetables are cooked, about 20 to 30 minutes.

Using a slotted spoon, remove the corn and the chile pepper. Transfer the remaining mixture to a blender, blend until smooth, then return to the stockpot.

Wash the spinach and remove the stalks. Bundle the leaves together and cut them into fine strips. Place the spinach strips in the stock and boil until spinach is cooked, about 5 minutes. Return the corn to the pot and simmer for another minute or two. Serve hot.

Variation: You can add either pieces of cooked peeled shrimp (green prawns) or strips of cooked skinless chicken breast, seasoned with black pepper, lime or lemon juice, and salt when you return the corn to the pot. Simmer for a further 3 or 4 minutes and serve.

SERVES 4

Roasted Breadfruit

Breadfruit is eaten throughout the Caribbean, enjoyed in many different ways in addition to this simple preparation. When cooked, the flesh is soft, white, and chewy like freshly baked white bread. A very dear, shy old Carib lady from Dominica told me that they call breadfruit *yampen woti* (yam bread). I thought at the time how close the name sounded to *yam,* which is fitting considering that both vegetables serve virtually the same function—they are usually eaten as the carbohydrates with main meals. Roasted breadfruit is wonderful served hot with stews, roasts, or grilled foods—anywhere you would use potatoes. It's delicious buttered and eaten by itself, or in the Breadfruit and Avocado Salad on page 43.

1 large breadfruit
   (approximately 2
   pounds/1 kg)
½ cup (113 g) butter
   (optional)
Salt and freshly ground
   black pepper to taste
Chopped parsley leaves,
   for garnish

This recipe is best made using a coal fire or an outdoor open fire, but failing that you can always roast it in a conventional oven. Preheat the oven to 400°F (200°C/gas mark 6).

Wash and dry the breadfruit. Using a skewer, make a couple of holes at either end of the breadfruit. Roast it in the coals of a hot fire or in the oven for about 1 to 1½ hours, turning at half-hour intervals to ensure even cooking. To check if it is cooked, slice out a sliver of the breadfruit; the inside should be soft and doughy, like freshly baked white bread.

Remove breadfruit from the fire or oven. Leave to cool for about 10 minutes, then use a big barbecue fork to hold it firmly and cut off the skin with a sharp knife to reveal the cooked flesh inside.

Slice the breadfruit and arrange it in a serving dish. Melt the butter and pour it over the breadfruit. Season with salt and pepper, sprinkle with chopped parsley, and serve hot.

SERVES 4

Breadfruit and jackfruit are related species, and many people get them mixed up because they are similar in looks and in their Southeast Asian origin. Jackfruit grow on stalks close to the bark of the tree while breadfruit grow in clusters, often hanging away from the parent tree. And unlike breadfruit, jackfruit can be eaten raw or cooked.

Breadfruit and Avocado Salad

The version of this salad I ate in Dominica was plain and unpretentious—just the avocado and the thin slices of baked breadfruit doused with the citrus dressing and garnished with fresh chopped herbs. But I like tender salad shoots as well as herbs, so I have added them in this recipe.

1 two-pound (907 g)
   breadfruit, roasted
   (see page 42)
2 avocados
Juice of 1 lemon

DRESSING
¼ cup (59 mL) light olive
   oil or corn oil
Juice of 1 lime
¼ cup (59 mL) white
   wine vinegar
Freshly ground black
   pepper to taste
Freshly ground sea salt
   to taste
4 ounces (113 g) bean
   sprouts
2 ounces (57 g) mixed
   green shoots, such as
   watercress or
   sunflower shoots

After roasting the breadfruit according to the instructions on page 42, allow it to cool to room temperature. Then peel and dice the flesh. Peel the avocados, remove the stones, dice the flesh, and squeeze over the lemon juice. In a salad bowl, toss the breadfruit and avocado together.

Combine the oil, lime juice, vinegar, pepper, and salt in a jar, shake well, and pour over the avocado and breadfruit mix. Sprinkle the sprouts and shoots over and toss the salad once more. Cover and leave at room temperature for approximately 1 hour before serving.

SERVES 4

Green Bananas in Curried Cream Sauce

I ate many mouthwatering foods with Loye Barnard at her relaxing holiday haven, perched 1,000 feet above the sea at Soufrière with the stunning views of Martinique and the meeting of two great waters, the Caribbean Sea and the Atlantic Ocean. Here then is my attempt at creating Loye's banana masterpiece so that you can evoke the atmosphere of delightful Dominica in your home. The "banana" used in this dish is actually green plantain, but a lot of people still refer to plantains as bananas because they look alike and belong to the same genus. However, unlike bananas, plantains are used mostly as vegetables. They taste best when cooked, not eaten raw like bananas. Serve this dish hot, with a green salad to accompany.

8 to 10 small green
   bananas or 4 large
   semiripe plantains
½ cup (113 g) butter
½ cup (85 g) all-purpose
   (plain) flour
1 tablespoon curry
   powder
5 cups (1.2 L) lowfat,
   canned evaporated
   milk
Salt and freshly ground
   pepper for seasoning
Pinch of freshly grated
   nutmeg
1 each small green and
   red bell peppers
   (capsicums), seeded
   and finely chopped
2 tablespoons grated,
   toasted fresh or
   desiccated coconut
Parsley sprigs, for garnish

Preheat the oven to 450°F (230°C/gas mark 8).

Peel the bananas and cut them into thick rounds. Place the bananas in a saucepan of boiling salted water and boil until tender, about 15 minutes. Drain and set aside.

Melt the butter in a heavy-bottomed saucepan or skillet over medium heat and stir in the flour and curry powder to make a roux. Cook, stirring with a wooden spoon, for 1 or 2 minutes. Warm up the milk separately until lukewarm, and pour it all at once into the roux. Stir until the sauce is smooth and thick. Season with salt and pepper and add the nutmeg.

Arrange the bananas in a baking dish and pour over the sauce. Sprinkle with the capsicum.

Bake for about 30 minutes. Remove from the oven and sprinkle with the toasted coconut. Garnish with parsley and serve hot.

SERVES 4 AS A SIDE DISH

Chicken Sankotch
SEASONED CHICKEN IN COCONUT CREAM

I had been told by Tom, a proud Dominican guide and driver, that it is not common to see local men cook, so it was with some amazement that I watched young Jones Peltier, looking perfectly at home in Loye Barnard's kitchen at Petit Coulibri, cook a most delicious chicken *sankotch* for dinner. Jones explained that the method of adding coconut to the chicken is what gives it the name *sankotch,* and that he had learned this variation of a local dish by working for the versatile Loye. The chicken is marinated overnight before use. Serve this dish with plain rice or Plantain Fried Rice (page 40) and a green salad. (Pictured opposite page 36.)

3 pounds (1.4 kg) boned chicken (preferably thigh meat)
2 scallions (spring onions), washed and finely chopped
3 cloves garlic, finely chopped
1 onion, finely chopped
1 Scotch bonnet chile (chilli), seeded and finely chopped (add extra if you like very hot food)
1 tablespoon mild curry powder
1 stick celery, washed and finely chopped (optional)
Leaves from 3 or 4 sprigs thyme (optional)
Salt and freshly ground pepper for seasoning
Flesh of 1 whole coconut
Sprig of parsley for garnish

Place the chicken pieces in a bowl with the scallions, garlic, onion, chile, curry powder, celery, thyme, and salt and pepper. Stir together to mix, cover, and store in the refrigerator overnight.

To make the coconut cream, break the coconut flesh into pieces and grate it finely. Save 1 tablespoon of the grated coconut for garnish. Place remaining coconut in the bowl of a food processor or blender and add 4 cups (946 mL) of water. Process until the coconut is totally liquefied, pour the liquid into a jug and let it stand until it separates, about 10 to 15 minutes. Strain off the resulting coconut cream and reserve 1 cup of the residual water.

Place the seasoned chicken and vegetables in a large saucepan and add the reserved coconut water. Bring to a boil, then reduce heat and simmer for about 20 minutes, or until tender. Add the coconut cream and simmer over a low heat for a further 50 to 60 minutes.

Adjust the salt and pepper seasoning. Add more chopped Scotch bonnet chile if desired. Toast the reserved 1 tablespoon of grated coconut in a small, dry frying pan over a low heat.

Put the chicken mixture into a serving dish, sprinkle over the toasted coconut, and garnish with parsley. Serve at once.

SERVES 4 AS A MAIN DISH

"Ground Provisions" and Shrimp au Gratin

In my quest to discover the changes that have occurred to familiar African produce since it left the shores of the mother continent, and how the foods have become more or less exotic, this simple recipe would have to be at the root of it all—if you will pardon the pun. Ground provisions include the root vegetables of yam, taro, sweet potato, potato, and cassava, as well as pumpkins. Serve hot with a green salad to accompany; it's also delicious cold.

6 cups (1.4 L) coconut milk

8 ounces (227 g) taro, peeled, washed, and thinly sliced

8 ounces (227 g) cassava, peeled, washed, and thinly sliced

8 ounces (227 g) potatoes, peeled, washed, and thinly sliced

8 ounces (227 g) pumpkin, peeled, washed, and thinly sliced

8 ounces (227 g) sweet potato, peeled, washed, and thinly sliced

8 ounces (227 g) yams (or additional sweet potato, if yams unavailable), peeled, washed, and thinly sliced

⅓ cup (85 g) butter

½ cup (118 mL) corn oil

Preheat the oven to 350°F (180°C/gas mark 4).

Pour the coconut milk into a large stockpot and bring to a boil. Add all the root vegetables, lower to medium heat, and simmer for just 3 to 5 minutes. Let stand for 5 minutes, strain off the coconut milk and save it.

In another large saucepan, melt butter and heat the oil. Sauté the shrimp and garlic together over a medium to high heat until the water has evaporated from the shrimp, about 15 to 20 minutes.

Remove the shrimp from the pan and set aside. Add the cornstarch to the hot oil, and stir with a wooden spoon to make a smooth roux. Add the saved coconut milk, and stir continuously until smooth. Add the Cheddar and continue to stir. Season with salt and pepper. If necessary, pour the cheese sauce into a blender, and blend on medium speed until absolutely smooth.

2 pounds (907 g) large,
   uncooked shrimp
   (prawns), peeled and
   deveined
2 cloves garlic, finely
   chopped

^{2}/$_3$ cups (113 g)
   cornstarch (cornflour)
11 ounces (312 g)
   Cheddar cheese, grated
Salt and freshly ground
   pepper to taste
1 ounce (28 g) Parmesan
   cheese

Grease a large baking dish. Arrange alternate layers of
cooked root vegetables and shrimp. Pour the cheese sauce
over the final layer, sprinkle with Parmesan, and bake in the
oven, uncovered, for 20 to 30 minutes. Serve hot with a
green salad.

SERVES 6 TO 8 AS A MAIN DISH

"Mountain chicken" is the name given to what many consider to be
Dominica's national delicacy: a huge toad found only in Dominica,
which is hunted for food. *Crapaud* stew is a (very) local specialty. My first
experience with *crapaud* was shared with Joyce and André Charles, in the
village of Soufrière in Dominica. To this day, I smile at the image of André
and myself, he an expert, I a keen novice, wandering through his farm at
night, flashlights in hand, looking for mountain chickens. We could hear
them and occasionally see them, but we couldn't seem to catch them.
Eventually, André successfully did the job on his own, and with the aid of
Joyce's culinary touch, we ate very well.

Curried Parrot Fish

What an exotic name for a fish! But when you see this beautifully colored fish, it's easy to understand where the name came from. Its colors make the parrot fish look like a prop for an interior design, or as if it belongs in an aquarium to be admired. Parrot fish can be cooked any way you would cook snapper. Serve with Plantain Fried Rice (page 40), fried pappadams, toasted shredded coconut to sprinkle over, and chutneys of your choice.

3 limes

4 parrot fish, about 3 pounds (1.4 kg) total, cleaned and scaled, or substitute snapper

Salt for seasoning

1 cup (237 mL) corn or vegetable oil

4 onions, finely chopped

3 cloves garlic, finely chopped

2 tablespoons curry powder

2 Scotch bonnet chiles (chillies), cleaned and finely sliced

6 tomatoes, blanched, skins removed, and coarsely chopped

1 cup (237 mL) water

Freshly ground pepper to taste

4 sprigs cilantro (fresh coriander), leaves only, for garnish

Cut the limes into quarters and rub the cut sides over the fish. Sprinkle with salt and cover. Leave to marinate for about 30 minutes. Drain off the marinade from the fish and save it.

Heat the oil in a large frying pan over a medium heat, and fry the fish until golden on both sides. Remove the fish and keep warm. Drain off any excess oil, leaving just a little to coat the bottom of the pan.

Add the onions and garlic and cook, stirring, until the onions start to brown. Add the curry powder and chile, stir briskly for a few seconds, and quickly add the tomato, marinade, and water. Season to taste with salt and pepper and simmer over a low heat for 2 minutes.

Return the fish to the pan, making sure that the sauce has covered each fish. Partially cover and simmer until the fish has softened and the sauce has thickened, about 15 to 20 minutes. Serve hot, garnished with the cilantro.

SERVES 4

Cocoa Creams

Say *"Theobroma cacao,"* or the more common name cocoa, and most people immediately think of the dark powder used to make chocolates, chocolate biscuits, ice creams, and drinks. Few people realize that the tree was first grown by the Aztecs, and that it was not until the middle of the nineteenth century that cocoa beans were first used to produce chocolate.

2 cups (473 mL) hot, thick drinking chocolate
1 tablespoon granulated gelatin
½ cup (113 g) superfine (caster) sugar
2 tablespoons Dominican rum, or other good quality white rum
1 tablespoon chocolate liqueur
1 cup (237 mL) heavy (double) cream
4 graham crackers or sweet digestive biscuits, coarsely crushed
4 sprigs mint, for garnish

Pour the hot chocolate into a large mixing bowl, sprinkle the gelatin over the top, and stir until dissolved. Add the sugar, the rum, and the liqueur, and stir well. Allow to stand until the mixture has cooled down. In a separate bowl, whip the cream until soft peaks form. Fold the cream into the chocolate mixture using the low speed on the blender, or by hand.

Place the graham cracker crumbs in the base of 4 individual dessert glasses and spoon the chocolate into the glasses. Refrigerate until set. Serve cold, garnished with sprigs of mint.

SERVES 4

MAKING CHOCOLATE BALLS FOR CHOCOLATE TEA

The coated beans are removed from the cocoa pods and fermented in bags for about a week. This process releases some juice, which can be used to make cocoa vinegar or discarded. The beans are then laid out to dry in the sun. Once dried, which can take anything from a few days to a couple of weeks, they are graded if they are to be exported or sold; if not, they are dry-roasted in a cookpot over low to medium heat until they are browned all over and aromatic, then they are removed. They are then allowed to cool a little and pounded or processed together with an aromatic spice like nutmeg. The pounding results in a firm, smooth, shiny chocolate that is then carefully rolled into balls and stored until it is grated to make chocolate drinks, or as the locals refer to it, "chocolate tea."

Conky

SPICED CASSAVA
COOKED IN BANANA LEAVES

Masterline Eustache is a resourceful young Carib with sound ecological reasoning. On one side, his piece of land is just a few steps down from the main road; on the other side, it is bordered by a sheer precipice leading straight down to the rocky sea below. The view of the ocean from his place is magnificent. Masterline puts every inch of his land to ecological use, selling food he grows and artifacts he makes from a streetside stall. A man of few words, he does not need to talk, for his hands do the talking. They are busy, always busy, and they were still busy when I met Masterline in the Carib Territory of Dominica. He was making *conky*. I watched in admiration as his deft hands worked on tubers of cassava for the *conky*. He peeled, washed, grated, seasoned, cut, shaped, wrapped, and tied *conky* after *conky*, making it look easy. I resolved to try and make them in my own kitchen when I got back home. The following recipe is the end result. It is not quite like Masterline's, but then again, no one can make *conky* like Masterline.

You can use rice paper if banana leaves are not available. Served with a cool drink, *conkies* make a very good after-school snack for children. Cooked *conkies* are a bit of a surprise. They look firm, yet glutinous and translucent, and taste delicious and sweet. It takes a long time to eat a whole one. Many is the time I have threatened to use them as gob-stoppers for garrulous friends!

1 pound (454 g) cassava
¼ teaspoon freshly
   grated nutmeg
¼ teaspoon cinnamon
¼ teaspoon allspice
2 teaspoons freshly
   grated ginger
⅔ cup (151 g) sugar

Peel the cassava, rinse, and then grate the flesh very finely. Place in a large bowl with about 2 quarts (1.9 L) of water and soak for about 30 minutes to rinse off some of the starch. Strain the water from the cassava with muslin cloth. Repeat the soaking and straining process once more.

In a large bowl, combine the nutmeg, cinnamon, allspice, ginger, and sugar, and slowly stir in a little water until the mixture is a thick paste. Combine this seasoned paste with the strained cassava and mix thoroughly. The final consistency should be that of a soft dough. Flatten the dough into

10 to 12 twelve-inch (30-cm) squares of fresh banana leaf, ballisier leaf, or rice paper (see note) for wrapping

10 to 12 twelve-inch (30-cm) lengths of string, for tying the *conkies*

individual ½-inch- (1-cm-) thick oblongs about 2 by 4 inches (5 by 10 cm) in size. Wrap them individually with the banana or ballisier leaves, then tie each parcel firmly with strings, both vertically and horizontally.

Using a set of tongs, carefully lower the conkies into boiling water (allowing enough water to cover them all) and boil until the contents feel firm and upon inspection look translucent, about 40 to 50 minutes. I suggest you use one conky in the batch as a tester.

When cooked, remove the conkies from heat and drain off the water. Lift out the conkies and allow them to cool. Serve cold.

Note: Ballisier leaves are a local plant with large leaves similar to those of the banana. If banana leaves or ballisier leaves are unavailable, you can use rice paper instead. The cooking process differs accordingly. Wrap the conky individually in sheets of rice paper that have been brushed with olive oil. Oil the outside of the rice paper parcels as well and arrange them in a single layer so that they do not stick together when cooking. Cook in the microwave on High for 6 minutes.

MAKES 10 TO 12 CONKIES

Tickle Me Belly

PANCAKES WITH MANGOES IN LIQUEUR

This dish's sweet tickling starts in the taste buds and then continues down into your stomach. You feel like giving your tummy a little gentle tickle, like babies do when they are enjoying a good feed—hence the name. The filling is best made the day before it is required.

FILLING
2 large, ripe mangoes
1/4 cup (59 mL) mango liqueur (optional)
Finely grated zest of 2 limes
1/3 cup (75 g) superfine (caster) sugar

PANCAKES
1 cup (170 g) all-purpose (plain) flour
Pinch of salt
Pinch of nutmeg
2 eggs
1 1/3 cups (354 mL) milk
1 fresh lime, sliced into thin rounds, for garnish

To make the filling, peel the mangoes and slice off the flesh into a bowl. Discard the stones. Pour the liqueur over the mangoes (if using), then sprinkle with the lime zest and the superfine sugar. Cover and refrigerate overnight.

Sift the flour, salt, and nutmeg together into a bowl. Place the eggs and milk in a blender and blend on high speed until smooth, about 30 to 40 seconds. Reduce the speed to low and slowly pour in the flour. Blend until smooth. Transfer the pancake batter to a jug and allow to stand for about 30 minutes before you cook the pancakes.

Grease a small (8-inch/20-cm) nonstick frying pan with vegetable oil. Heat the pan over medium heat until hot, then pour about 3 tablespoons of the pancake batter into the hot pan. Swirl the pan round so that the batter evenly coats the bottom of the pan. Cook the pancake until it is golden on one side, about 1 to 1 1/2 minutes, then turn it over and cook the other side. Repeat the process with the remaining batter, keeping the cooked pancakes warm until all are cooked. The batter makes approximately 6 to 8 pancakes.

Put a spoonful of the filling onto each pancake, then fold over the pancake and put another spoonful of the filling on top. Garnish with slices of lime, and serve hot.

SERVES 4

Opposite: Skewered Fruits Baked with Curaçao (page 32)

Rum and Lime Ices

The tradition of growing, using, and exporting limes from Dominica goes back a long way. For many years, the limes for the English Rose's Lime Juice came from Dominica. It is therefore not unusual to find that lime plays an important role in Dominican food and drinks.

8 large limes or lemons
2 tablespoons granulated gelatin
2 tablespoons superfine (caster) sugar
2 cups (473 mL) lime cordial or limeade from frozen concentrate
¾ cup (177 mL) Dominican rum
Tropical flowers, for garnish (optional)

Cut the tops off the limes and save the tops to be used as lids later on. Using a sharp knife, cut around the inside of the peel to free the flesh, then use a spoon to scoop out all the flesh and leave the fruit cases empty and in shape. Set aside the cases and discard the flesh.

Combine the gelatin and sugar and stir. Put the lime juice cordial and rum into a blender, add the gelatin and sugar mix, and blend well on low speed. Pour the mixture into fruit cases and cover with the sliced-off fruit lids.

Stand the filled fruit cases in a tight-fitting dish in the freezer until set, about 1 to 2 hours. Serve garnished with your favorite flower either stuck into the ice under the lid or on the side.

SERVES 4

Hot Orange and Lime Toddy

I suspect this drink has its roots firmly in the slave era, when European settlers preferred their drinks hot—even in the heat of the Caribbean.

2 cups (473 mL) fresh orange juice
2 cups (473 mL) fresh lime juice
1 cup (227 g) superfine (caster) sugar
Pinch of allspice
6 cloves

Put all ingredients into a large stockpot or saucepan. Heat over a medium heat until hot. Lower the heat and simmer for 15 to 20 minutes, uncovered. Turn off the heat, cover, and leave to stand for 1 hour. When ready to serve, strain the mixture to remove the spices, then heat up the toddy and serve it warm or hot in cordial glasses with handles.

Variation: You can add a few thick slices of fresh ginger to the mixture before simmering.

SERVES 4

Opposite: Blue Lagoon (page 34)

GUADELOUPE

From the air, Guadeloupe is a symbol of romantic beauty. It looks just like a butterfly floating luxuriously in the blue waters of the Caribbean. Little wonder the original Amerindian inhabitants, the Arawaks, named the island Karukera, meaning "the island of beautiful waters."

Guadeloupe has a strong French influence. Through its famous *cuisinières* (formidable female master cooks), it can boast of the best Creole cuisine in the Caribbean. There are more than 300 of these fabulous lady cooks who together have formalized an association called *Le Cuistot Mutuel.* Founded on July 4, 1916, by gregarious descendants of early Creoles, the association pays tribute to Saint Lawrence, the patron saint of the *cuisinières.* St. Lawrence was a deacon who became a martyr in the year 258 after he was reportedly burned alive on a grill of hot coals (barbecued!).

This tribute lasts for one week and takes place in the form of an annual *Cuisinières* Festival held every August in Pointe à Pitre. During the week, many activities take place around food: its gathering and preparation, and the reaffirmation of the cooks' solidarity. Each year, a new fabric for the cooks' dresses is chosen by the association, to be worn under their specially designed aprons covered in cooking motifs that are appliquéd around the name of St. Lawrence.

Early in the week, a remembrance mass is held for the souls of departed *cuisinières*, before the serious preparations commence for the final day's climax of abundant food taken into the church for blessings during the mass in honor of St. Lawrence. The final day of the week is reserved for the spectacular carnival of food—a stunning array of Creole specialties, painstakingly cooked and carried by the *cuisinières* themselves from their homes to the local basilica. After the service, the food is again carried out by the *cuisinières* amid singing and dancing in a colorful procession through the streets to a final feasting hall, where, for a nominal fee, the food is shared with all. It is truly a stunning festival to behold. I had the good fortune to attend one. It was spectacular and I ate far too much!

Christophenes Farcies
STUFFED CHAYOTES

Thought to belong to the gourd family, chayote, or christophene, is a kind of bland-tasting squash, originally from Mexico and very popular in the Caribbean, although it is also eaten in other countries. It goes by many names besides chayote and christophene, including *choko, cho-cho, choyote,* and squash. Here are some alternative stuffing suggestions and, of course, you can always make up your own fancy fillings. For instance, you may choose to sauté some chicken or pork sausage, with fresh herbs such as chives, shallots, scallions (spring onions), or parsley. (Pictured opposite page 21.)

2 large chayotes
(christophenes)
1/4 cup (59 mL) vegetable
oil
1 onion, finely chopped
1 clove garlic, chopped
1 carrot, finely diced
1 red or yellow Scotch
bonnet chile (chilli),
finely chopped
Salt to taste
4 ounces (113 g) soft
bread crumbs
4 ounces (113 g) finely
grated Cheddar or
cheese of your choice
1 tablespoon fresh thyme
leaves

Wash the chayotes, dry them, and cut each one into two, so you have four halves. Core each half and discard the core.

In about 6 cups (1.4 L) of boiling water, cook the chayote halves without allowing them to get too soft, about 30 minutes. This is primarily to make the flesh inside soft enough to scoop out.

Meanwhile, preheat the oven to 400°F (200°C/gas mark 6).

Heat the oil in a heavy-bottomed frying pan or skillet over a low heat and sauté the onion, garlic, carrot, and chile for about 3 minutes. Remove from the heat and set aside.

Remove the chayote halves from the water. Use a knife to score three or four lines vertically and horizontally in the flesh without piercing the outer skin. Use a spoon to scoop out as much of the flesh as possible. Save the cases, and add the pulp to the mixture in the frying pan.

Place the pan over a medium heat, stir well to mix, season with salt to taste and continue to sauté the filling for a further 5 minutes, stirring all the time to avoid burning. Remove from the heat, divide the filling into four, and fill each chayote case.

In a small bowl, combine the bread crumbs, cheese, and thyme, and evenly sprinkle the mixture over the tops of the filled cases. Arrange the filled chayote halves on a baking sheet and bake in the preheated oven for 10 to 15 minutes. Serve hot either as a light meal or as an appetizer.

SERVES 4 AS AN APPETIZER OR SIDE DISH

Saltfish and Shrimp Bake

The salt cod needs to be soaked overnight prior to use. You may substitute an equal weight of cooked, flaky white-fleshed fish.

1 pound (454 g) salt cod
½ cup (118 mL) olive oil
2 onions, finely diced
2 cloves garlic, finely chopped
2 Scotch bonnet chiles, seeded and finely chopped
1 eggplant (aubergine), peeled and finely diced
4 potatoes, peeled and sliced into thin rounds
2 cups (43 g) fresh parsley leaves
5 ounces (142 g) cabbage, finely shredded
8 ounces (227 g) pumpkin, peeled and finely diced
8 ounces (227 g) large, uncooked shrimp (prawns), peeled, deveined, and finely diced
Juice of 1 lemon
Salt and freshly ground pepper to taste

Soak the salt cod overnight in lots of cold water. The next day, rinse thoroughly to get rid of most of the salt. Taste a piece of the fish to test for saltiness. If it is still salty, rinse the fish several times under cold running water or soak it for a further 1 to 2 hours, then rinse. When you reach your desired level of saltiness, remove the skin from the back of the fish and use a knife to flake the flesh into many small pieces, taking care to remove all the bones.

Preheat the oven to 375°F (190°C/gas mark 5).

In a large frying pan or skillet, heat half the olive oil over a low to medium heat, then sauté the onion, garlic, chiles, eggplant, and the fish flakes for about 10 to 15 minutes, or until the vegetables are soft.

Grease a medium to large baking dish. Arrange ingredients in layers as follows: start with half the potatoes, then all the cod and onion mixture, half of the parsley, the cabbage, pumpkin, and shrimp. Drizzle with a little lemon juice.

For the final layer, arrange the remaining half of the potatoes on top and sprinkle them with the remaining parsley. Season with salt and pepper and drizzle the remaining olive oil over the dish. Cover with aluminum foil and bake in the oven for 45 minutes to 1 hour, or until all the ingredients are cooked and soft. Remove the foil before the last 20 minutes of cooking time. Serve hot as a main meal.

SERVES 4

Fish Mousse

This is a spectacular dish, so give it center stage on a large plate. Turning it out of a large fish mold can be a little tricky, but smaller molds are not as visually spectacular. Serve cold with a salad of your choice, or hot out of the oven, sliced, with Parmesan cheese sprinkled over.

$^1/_2$ cup (118 mL) white wine

1 cup (237 mL) coconut milk

2 shallots, peeled and finely chopped

2 cloves garlic, finely chopped

2 celery stalks, finely chopped

$^1/_2$ teaspoon chile (chilli) powder

1 green bell pepper (capsicum), seeded and finely chopped

1 tablespoon tomato purée

1 one-pound (454 g) smoked tuna or mackerel fillet

Salt and freshly ground pepper to taste

2 egg whites

In a large saucepan, combine the wine, coconut milk, shallots, garlic, celery, chile powder, bell pepper, and tomato purée and slowly bring to a boil over a medium heat.

Use a knife to remove all the flesh from the fish, then check for and discard any bones. Flake the fish and add it to the contents of the saucepan. Stir the mixture and continue to boil it until the liquid has reduced by about half, about 10 to 15 minutes. Remove from the heat and set aside to cool. Taste and season accordingly.

While this mixture is cooling, preheat oven to 350°F (180°C/gas mark 4).

Beat the egg whites until they form stiff peaks. Purée the fish mixture in a blender and then fold it in to the egg whites. Grease a large mold (preferably fish shaped) and pour in the mixture. Cook uncovered in the center of the oven for 50 to 60 minutes, or until set. Cook for a further 15 minutes, increasing the heat to 425°F (220°C/gas mark 7). Remove from the oven and allow to cool at room temperature, then refrigerate for 2 hours or so, until more firmly set, before you unmold.

Just before you unmold the mousse, dip the base of the mold in boiling water. Totally cover the top of the mold with an appropriately sized oval serving plate. Quickly invert the mousse onto the plate. Serve cold.

SERVES 4 AS A MAIN DISH

Crabes Farcis
STUFFED CRABS

August is the season for land crabs in Guadeloupe. Young boys catch them, string a few together, and sell them on the side of the road. The *cuisinières* (the matriarchs of Guadeloupean Creole cooking) take this opportunity to create some exquisite crab dishes during *La Fête des Cuisinières,* or the Cooks' Festival, which happens annually in August. *Crabes farcis* is one of their many Creole specialties.

Juice of 3 large lemons

1 teaspoon salt

4 land crabs or other medium-sized crabs, or equivalent weight of frozen crab meat plus four crab shells (see sidebar)

6 sprigs of thyme, stalks removed

2 cups (85 g) soft bread crumbs

2 tablespoons finely chopped fresh parsley

1½ cups (355 mL) coconut milk

⅓ cup (78 mL) corn or olive oil

2 large onions, finely chopped

2 tablespoons chopped fresh chives

6 cloves garlic, finely chopped

Bring about 2 quarts (1.9 L) water to boil in a large Dutch oven or stockpot. Add the juice of 1 lemon and the 1 teaspoon salt. Meanwhile, stun the live crabs (if using) by placing them in the freezer or in a bath of ice water. When water has boiled, carefully drop the crabs in the boiling water. Return the water to a boil and continue to boil for about 5 minutes. Remove the crabs from the water using a slotted spoon, retaining the water in the pot, and place the crabs under cold running water to cool them down.

Now cut 2 lemons into quarters and use them to thoroughly clean the crabs by rubbing their surfaces with the cut lemons.

Return the crabs to the water, add half the thyme, and boil for a further 5 to 10 minutes, or until their color changes. Carefully remove the crabs from the water and cool enough to handle. Remove the shells and scoop out any crab juices and soft meat inside the shells. Save this and the shells. Remove the rest of the crabmeat from the legs and the main body and reserve.

In a separate bowl, soak the bread crumbs, the remaining thyme, and the parsley in the coconut milk.

1 Scotch bonnet chile (chilli), or other hot chile, seeded and finely chopped
Salt and freshly ground pepper to taste
2 tablespoons (28 g) butter
2 ounces (57 g) Parmesan cheese (optional)

In a heavy-bottomed frying pan or skillet, heat the oil over a medium heat and sauté the onions, chives, garlic, and chile for about 3 minutes. Stir in all the crabmeat and continue to cook for another 3 minutes. Add the bread crumb mixture and continue to cook for a further 3 minutes. Season with salt and pepper to taste.

Preheat the oven to 350°F (180°C/gas mark 4).

Fill the reserved crab shells with the bread crumb and crabmeat mixture. Press the tops down with the back of a spoon so that they are smooth. Cut the butter into 4 slivers and place one on top of each stuffed crab. Sprinkle each shell with Parmesan (if using). Arrange on a baking sheet and bake in the oven for 20 to 30 minutes, depending on the size of the crab shells. Serve hot.

SERVES 4 AS AN APPETIZER

Some people are squeamish about killing live crabs. If you are of that persuasion, I suggest you use frozen crabmeat and buy separate crab shells for this recipe. Follow the instructions from when the crabmeat is extracted from the boiled crabs. Prior to baking the stuffed crab shells in the oven, you may choose to do what I do sometimes, which is to sprinkle a little bit of Parmesan over the top of each filled crab shell. It gives it a nice firm, golden crust and makes it an aesthetically pleasing dish.

Blaff
CARIBBEAN FISH SOUP

I think it is fair to say I have *blaffed* my way around the Caribbean. I consumed this wonderful fish soup like there was no tomorrow. You know how it is—you eat something so tasty in one country and become obsessed by it, so that any time you see it on a menu somewhere else, you head straight for it again? Well, that's how it was with me and *blaff*. I first tasted it when I found myself seriously involved in the art of "liming," or taking it easy, on Las Cuervas beach in Trinidad, and Joseph, a generous local limer, cooked *blaff* for me. Perhaps it was the environment and not just the cooking but whatever it was, the *blaff* that day was just so delightful and addictive! That was the beginning of my problem, but I didn't *really* get hooked until I tasted this Guadeloupean version. The name *blaff* is said to represent the sound the fish makes when it hits the hot soup broth.

2 lemons

1½ pounds (680 g) fresh mackerel fillet, in 4 pieces

1 small bunch fresh thyme, sprigs broken into small pieces

2 onions, finely chopped

4 sprigs parsley, broken into small pieces

2 cloves garlic, coarsely chopped

2 Scotch bonnet chiles (chillies)

½ bunch chives, finely chopped

1 bouquet garni (see page 142)

Salt and freshly ground pepper

2 tablespoons (30 mL) aromatic olive oil (olive oil flavored with herbs)

Cut one of the lemons in half and rub the cut halves over the fish to clean it. Cut the second lemon in half and reserve half for a garnish. Place the fish in a bowl. Marinate by adding the juice from the lemon half, and half the thyme, 1 onion, half the parsley, half the garlic, 1 chile, and half the chives. Stir well so that the marinade thoroughly coats the fish. Cover and allow to stand in a cool place for 2 to 3 hours.

In a large stockpot, bring about 2 quarts (1.9 L) of water to a boil. Add the bouquet garni, the remaining thyme, onion, parsley, garlic, chile, and chives, and a little salt and freshly ground pepper. Allow to boil vigorously for about 5 minutes. Take care to remove the chile.

Carefully add the marinade (not the fish), return to a boil, and boil for 5 to 10 minutes, so the flavors of the herbs can infuse the water. Add the fish (and listen for the sound of "blaffing"). Lower the heat and simmer for a further 10 minutes, or until fish is tender and cooked.

To serve, place a piece of fish in each warmed soup bowl, ladle out some of the broth and spoon it over the fish. Drizzle a little oil and lemon juice over each dish and serve hot.

SERVES 4

Spicy Cream of Pumpkin Soup

Pumpkin is one of the vegetables I saw used most often in the Caribbean. The thick-skinned vegetables with vivid yellow insides are everywhere in the Caribbean. They are so fresh and sweet, it is little wonder they are so popular in many local dishes. This one is a simple soup with a spicy touch.

¼ cup (57 g/59 mL) butter or vegetable oil

2 cloves garlic, finely chopped

1 small onion, finely chopped

1 teaspoon seeded, chopped Scotch bonnet chile (chilli)

1 teaspoon grated fresh ginger

½ teaspoon cinnamon

½ teaspoon powdered saffron

¼ teaspoon allspice

4 cups (946 mL) coconut milk

2 cups (473 mL) vegetable stock

Salt and freshly ground pepper to taste

2 carrots, cleaned and chopped into bite-sized chunks

4 pounds (1.8 kg) pumpkin, peeled, seeded, and cut into bite-sized chunks

4 to 6 sprigs parsley, for garnish

2 tablespoons (30mL) light (single) cream, for garnish

In a large, heavy-bottomed saucepan, melt the butter or heat the oil over a medium heat and sauté the garlic, onion, and chile until the onion looks transparent, about 3 to 5 minutes.

Stir in the spices and the coconut milk [or stock (if using)]. Season with salt and pepper to taste. Bring to the boil and simmer for 3 to 4 minutes. Add the carrots and pumpkin, partially cover the pan, and bring the mixture to the boil. Cook over a low heat until the vegetables are soft and cooked, about 40 to 50 minutes.

Remove from the heat, leave to cool down a little (about 10 minutes), then purée in a blender until smooth. Return the soup to the pot to gently heat through. Do not allow the soup to boil.

When the soup is heated through, remove the pan from the heat and ladle equal quantities into warmed soup bowls. Place a small, decorative sprig of parsley in the center of each bowl and swirl a little cream in a small circle around the parsley. Serve hot with bread.

SERVES 4 TO 6

Bébélé

SEASONED BREADFRUIT AND VEGETABLE SOUP WITH PORK AND DUMPLINGS

At the risk of sounding frivolous, I have to say that whenever I hear the word *bébélé* I feel like breaking into a dance. It sounds more like the name of an African dance than a meal. However, *bébélé* is a Creole dish that comes from the French Caribbean islands, such as Guadeloupe, Martinique, Marie Galante, Îles des Saintes and Désiderade. It is a tasty, hearty, predominantly vegetable soup—a very clever way of making a little go far. It appears to have its origins in the iniquitous slave times. If *bébélé* has a fault, it is that it is tasty without being colorful, but don't let that stop you enjoying it. I have added a little saffron and paprika to the dumplings for color.

8 ounces (227 g) boneless smoked ham hock, cut into cubes, or one pig's tail (optional)
Pinch of salt
1 large sprig celery with leaves, cleaned and finely chopped
½ of a ripe breadfruit, peeled, cored, and cut into 1-inch (2.5-cm) cubes
12 ounces (340 g) pumpkin, peeled and cut into 1-inch (2.5-cm) cubes
4 cloves garlic, finely chopped
Leaves from 2 sprigs thyme

If using a pig's tail, wash and chop it into 2-inch (5-cm) lengths. Bring about 1 quart (946 mL) of water to a boil, add salt and the pig's tail, and cook until the tail is soft but not completely cooked, about 20 minutes. Discard the water and reserve the pig's tail. If you are using smoked ham hock, then just rinse it under cold running water.

In a large Dutch oven or saucepan, put the meat (if using), the celery, breadfruit, pumpkin, and half the garlic, and about 1 quart (946 mL) of water. Bring to a boil and simmer slowly for about 30 minutes.

Meanwhile, make the dumplings. Combine the flour, salt, baking powder, and saffron and paprika if using, in a bowl. Stir to mix well. Make a well in the center and slowly add small amounts of lukewarm water to form a solid dough—not too soft, not too hard, just firm to the touch. Add more flour or water as needed. Pinch off small portions of the dough (about the size of a large cherry). Roll the dough on your palm to form it into round balls and set aside.

1 sprig lemon1 scented
thyme
1 small bunch chives,
finely chopped
1 teaspoon saffron
powder or ground
turmeric
Juice of 1 lemon
1 whole fresh Scotch
bonnet or habanero
chile (chilli)
Parsley, for garnish

DUMPLINGS
MAKES APPROXIMATELY
20 TO 25

2 cups (340 g) all-purpose
(plain) flour
Pinch of salt
1 teaspoon baking
powder
$\frac{1}{2}$ teaspoon saffron
powder (optional)
$\frac{1}{2}$ teaspoon paprika
(optional)

Add the other half of the garlic, the thyme, chives, saffron, lemon juice, the dumplings, and the chile to the vegetables. Do not crush the chile. Stir and simmer for a further 1 to 1$\frac{1}{2}$ hours, or until the dumplings and vegetables are soft and the meat is cooked. The consistency should be thick and the vegetables largely mashed up. Remove the chile. Serve soup in warmed individual bowls or in a large serving bowl, garnished with parsley.

SERVES 4 AS A MAIN DISH

Smoked Fish and Avocado Salad

Growing up in Africa, we almost always used avocado as a spread or sandwich filling. The fruit itself was referred to locally as pears. When I arrived in England many years ago, I found that pears were something quite different. Everybody referred to my brand of pears as avocados. The confusion was quite hilarious at times. I was therefore both surprised and gratified to discover that many islands in the Caribbean also refer to avocados as pears and have turned them into exotic masterpieces like hot pear soup and pear ice cream. Serve the salad as an appetizer or toss in with freshly cooked pasta or steamed brown rice.

10 ounces (283 g) smoked fish fillets, such as mackerel or tuna
1 small onion, finely chopped into rings
1 clove garlic, finely chopped
Juice from 1 lemon
1 tablespoon (15 mL) light olive oil
2 large avocados
Salt and freshly ground black pepper
Small bunch cilantro (fresh coriander), without roots and finely chopped

Remove the skin from the fish. Cut the flesh into small chunks and carefully remove all traces of bone from the fish. Set aside.

Combine the onion rings with the garlic, lemon juice, and oil and leave to stand for 30 minutes. Peel the avocados and discard the stones. Cut the avocado flesh into cubes and toss the cubes in with the onion and lemon mix, making sure that the lemon marinade coats the avocado cubes.

Combine the avocado mix with the fish chunks. Sprinkle with salt, pepper, and the finely chopped coriander. Toss together as a salad, taste for saltiness, adjust seasoning accordingly, and serve.

Variation: If you find the smoked fish too salty—or if you simply prefer more vegetables in the dish—add 1 cup each finely chopped celery leaves, zucchini, and tomato.

SERVES 4 AS A SIDE DISH

Papaya et Legume au Gratin
PAPAYA AND VEGETABLES WITH CHEESE

Once upon a time, unripe green papaya held status only among medicine men and women of the tropics and a handful of traditional cooks. Since science discovered it is a good protein tenderizer, it has become fashionable and papaya recipes are springing up all over the place. The race is on to see who comes up with the most interesting and original recipe! Serve hot as a main meal or as an accompaniment to meat or fish dishes. (Pictured between pages 68 and 69.)

1 green papaya
2 zucchini (courgettes)
2 tablespoons (28 g) butter
¼ cup (59 mL) extra virgin olive oil
1 onion, finely chopped
2 cloves garlic, finely chopped
3 scallions (spring onions), finely chopped
½ cup (85 g) cornstarch (cornflour)
2 cups (473 mL) nonfat milk
Salt and freshly ground pepper to taste
13 ounces (369 g) lowfat, sharp Cheddar cheese, grated
1 teaspoon mild curry powder
4 cups (113 g) soft bread crumbs, loosely packed

Preheat the oven to 400°F (200°C/gas mark 6).

Carefully cut the papaya in half and scoop out the seeds. Peel off the skin and cut the flesh into 1-inch (2.5-cm) cubes. Peel the zucchini and cut them into the same size pieces as the papaya.

In a large, heavy-bottomed saucepan or skillet, melt the butter and heat the oil over a medium heat. Add the onion, garlic, and scallions and sauté for about 4 to 5 minutes, until the onions are clear.

Sprinkle over the cornstarch and mix in, stirring with a wooden spoon. When the cornstarch is blended into a paste, add the milk and stir vigorously until the mixture is creamy and well blended. Add salt and pepper to taste. Now add half the cheese and continue to stir until it has melted and you have a smooth cheese sauce.

Remove from the heat and allow to cool slightly, then pour the sauce into a blender, and blend on medium to high until smooth and creamy. Set aside.

Grease a large baking dish and arrange the papaya and zucchini cubes in the base of the dish. Pour the cheese sauce over the vegetables.

In a small bowl, mix together the curry powder, the other half of the cheese, and the bread crumbs, and sprinkle the mixture over the dish. Bake for 20 to 25 minutes, or until the zucchini and papaya are cooked and soft and the crust is golden brown. Serve hot.

SERVES 4 AS A SIDE DISH

Lambi Colombo
CONCH CURRY

My first experience of *lambi* was not without its drama. I had arrived in Guadeloupe in a wheelchair and feeling quite low. Carolle, a beautiful young Guadeloupean woman, was designated to chaperone me around town. She wanted to cheer me up so she enlisted the help of her boyfriend, Patrice, to drive us to dinner. I did not know where we were going, it was in the middle of the hurricane season, a dark and rainy night, and we were late for dinner. The only person I have seen drive like Patrice did that night was paid handsomely for his efforts by a Formula One motor racing sponsor. Carolle and Patrice promised me the meal would be good and it was superb. It was *lambi* cooked to perfection by a chef in the Creole quarter. For days I could close my eyes and remember the flavors and atmosphere. Serve *lambi colombo* with cucumber salad and plain or curried long-grain rice (see sidebar).

2 pounds (907 g) conch or, if unavailable, abalone
6 lemons or limes
3 cups (710 mL) white wine, such as Riesling
Pinch of salt
3 cloves garlic, coarsely chopped, plus 2 cloves garlic, finely chopped
1 Scotch bonnet chile (chilli), seeded and finely sliced, plus 1 whole Scotch bonnet (optional)
2 bay leaves
1 large sprig basil
¼ cup (59 mL) oil
2 onions, peeled and finely sliced into rounds

Conch is very slippery and needs to be thoroughly cleaned. Fill a basin with cold water and place the conch in it. Cut the lemons in half and rub the conch with the cut halves. Make sure you change the water several times until the conch stops being so slippery.

Both conch and abalone need to be tenderized before use. Wrap the conch (or abalone) in a clean dishtowel and pound with a wooden kitchen mallet a few times.

After tenderizing, put the conch in a large saucepan and pour over the white wine. Add the pinch of salt, the three cloves of garlic, the whole chile (if using), the bay leaves, and the basil. Bring to a boil, and boil for about 30 minutes. Remove the chile and the bay leaves and set aside the wine stock and conch.

1 teaspoon saffron
  powder
1 tablespoon mild curry
  powder
1 bunch cilantro (fresh
  coriander), cleaned
  and stalks removed
4 large tomatoes,
  blanched, skin
  removed, and coarsely
  chopped
2 teaspoons tomato paste
Salt and freshly ground
  pepper

In a big skillet or saucepan, heat the oil and fry the onions, finely chopped garlic, and chopped chile for about 10 minutes, or until golden. Add the saffron, curry powder, half the cilantro, the tomato, tomato paste, and the conch and wine stock. Season to taste and allow to simmer slowly until sauce thickens and the conch is soft, about 30 to 40 minutes. Garnish with the remaining cilantro and serve.

SERVES 4 AS A MAIN DISH

CURRIED RICE

To make curried rice, you need previously cooked long-grain rice, chopped garlic, some butter, some olive oil, mild curry powder, and salt and freshly ground pepper. Melt the butter and heat the olive oil together in a pan. Lightly fry the garlic and add the curry powder and a dash of salt and pepper. Tip in the rice and stir vigorously to combine all the ingredients. To serve, form into molds by spooning the mixture into small pudding molds or teacups and packing tightly to take the shape of the container before you tip it out onto a plate.

Mango and Salt Cod Salad

This is a variation on a very interesting dish I tasted while filming in Guadeloupe. The taste was so sensational that it made a lasting impression on me and I vowed to experiment as soon as I returned home. The dish I enjoyed so much was hot and riddled with masses of mango and salt cod. I figured that a salad version would be just as exciting and it was—so here it is. Serve it with either hot garlic bread or fresh baguettes and butter as an appetizer, a light lunch, or as an accompaniment to main dishes. (Pictured opposite.)

4 ounces (113 g) salt cod
¼ cup (59 mL) extra
    virgin olive oil
Juice of 1 lime
Salt and freshly ground
    pepper to taste
2 tablespoons (30 mL)
    batterie (concentrated
    sugarcane juice) or 1
    tablespoon brown
    sugar dissolved in 2
    tablespoons water
4 medium to large
    semiripe mangoes,
    peeled, and the flesh
    cut into thin slivers
4 carrots, peeled and cut
    into thin matchsticks
1 cucumber, peeled and
    cut into thin
    matchsticks
1 red or green Scotch
    bonnet chile, seeded
    and cut into very thin
    strips
1 bunch lemon-scented
    thyme

Soak the salt cod overnight in lots of cold water. The next day, rinse thoroughly to get rid of most of the salt. Taste a piece of the fish to test for saltiness. If still salty, rinse several times under cold water or soak for a further 1 to 2 hours, then rinse.

When you reach your desired taste of saltiness, remove the skin from the back of the fish and use a knife to flake the flesh into many small pieces, taking care to remove all the bones.

Combine the oil, lime juice, salt and pepper, and batterie, and stir well to mix, then toss together with the mango, carrots, cucumber, and chile. Add the thyme last.

Cover and leave to stand for 1 to 2 hours before serving.

SERVES 4 AS A SIDE DISH

Following pages (clockwise from bottom left): Plantain Fried Rice (page 40); Spicy Plantain and Chicken Satay (page 127); Sauce Chien (page 70); Konkomber and Bean Salad (page 24); Trinidadian Lamb Curry (page 119); Salad Greens with Lime Dressing (page 25); Carig (page 120); Papaya et Legume au Gratin (page 65); Langoustes Grillées (page 70)

Bean and Breadfruit Ratatouille

Any time I travel between towns in the Caribbean and see the abundance of huge breadfruit pendulously hanging from the trees, I think of the story I read about the mutiny on the *Bounty*. If you don't know the story, it is reputed that breadfruit was the cause of the infamous mutiny. Captain Bligh, sailing between Tahiti and the Caribbean, was bringing back with him large numbers of breadfruit seedlings. The idea was to grow the breadfruit in the Caribbean and use the fruit to feed the slaves. There was a water shortage on this particular trip and the scarce liquid was rationed to all, but apparently the crew found out that Captain Bligh was using secret supplies to water his precious breadfruit. The crew mutinied. Serve the dish hot by itself or as an accompaniment to a roast dish or grilled fish or meat.

½ cup (113 mL) olive or corn oil, plus extra

1 large eggplant (aubergine), or 4 white eggplants, cleaned and cut into thick slices

1 one-pound (454 g) breadfruit, peeled, cored, and cut into small triangular pieces

1 large onion, chopped into thick slices

2 cloves garlic, finely chopped

6 large tomatoes, blanched, skin removed, and cut into chunks

2 large sprigs basil (use leaves only)

12 ounces (340 g) cooked black-eyed peas (beans)

1 Scotch bonnet chile (chilli)

Salt to taste

½ cup (113 mL) vegetable stock or water (optional)

In a large frying pan or skillet, heat the oil over a medium heat and fry the eggplant until golden. Remove and set aside. Add the breadfruit to the pan and cook it until golden. Remove and drain off half the oil.

Add a little more oil and fry the onion and garlic. Add the tomatoes, basil, black-eyed peas, chile, and the cooked eggplant and breadfruit. Stir together to mix, taking care not to crush the chile. Season to taste and if there is not enough liquid, add ½ cup (118 mL) vegetable stock or water.

Simmer over a low heat until the vegetables are cooked and soft, about 20 to 30 minutes. Before serving, remove the chile and save it to flavor something else if desired. Serve hot.

SERVES 4 AS A SIDE DISH

Opposite: Matété Antillean (page 72)

Langoustes Grillées avec Sauce Chien

GRILLED LOBSTERS WITH "DOG" SAUCE

Barbecues are part and parcel of today's lifestyle, and once we are in a barbecuing mood, we would, if we could, barbecue anything edible that we can get our hands on. Courtesy of diving friends, I have eaten lobster (crayfish) cooked this way on many occasions but never with a "dog" sauce! Madame Rosanne at La Cigalle, her restaurant in Basse Terre, on the Guadeloupean island of the same name, first introduced me to lobster with "dog" (actually, chopped vegetable) sauce. I was so impressed, I asked for the recipe, and after a few modifications of my own, here it is for your enjoyment also. The secret of the "dog" sauce is to mince the vegetables very, very finely; the chopping releases the full vegetable aromas so they can penetrate the sauce. I suggest you use a curved, double-handled chopping knife, commonly referred to as a *mahrata,* for this. It makes it easier, but if you haven't got a *mahrata,* use a large chopping knife on a big chopping board. Serve with a green salad and hot baked potatoes or seasoned rice if you like. (Pictured between pages 68 and 69.)

Juice of 2 limes
4 cloves garlic, finely
   chopped
¼ cup (59 mL) vegetable
   oil
Pinch of salt
2 lobsters, about 1 pound
   (454 g) each

SAUCE CHIEN
2 scallions (spring onions)
2 large sprigs parsley
1 small bunch celery
   leaves
2 sprigs thyme
2 onions

In a bowl, whisk together the juice of 2 limes with the garlic, vegetable oil, and salt.

Thoroughly clean your lobsters under cold running water, if necessary scrubbing them clean with cut lime halves as well, then cut the lobsters in half horizontally. Put them on a grill over a hot charcoal fire or barbecue, and grill for about 5 to 7 minutes. When the lobsters start to steam, brush the mixture of the combined lime juice, garlic, oil, and salt. over the lobster meat as it grills. Cook for a further 2 to 3 minutes.

While the lobster is grilling, prepare your *sauce chien.* Chop the scallions, parsley, and celery leaves very, very finely. Remove the leaves from the thyme, add them to the chopped parsley mixture, and chop again. Chop the onions and the chile very finely, add them to the chopped ingredients, and chop the whole lot again. Finely chop the garlic, add it to the parsley mixture, and chop again.

1 fresh hot chile (chilli),
   seeded
2 cloves garlic
Juice of 2 limes
2 tablespoons (30 mL)
   white vinegar
Salt
Freshly ground black
   pepper to taste
$^{1}/_3$ cup (78 mL) oil

Put all the chopped ingredients into a large mixing bowl with the lime juice, vinegar, and salt. Stir well to mix *before* you add the oil—this is part of the process of preparing yourself for the smell sensations to come. Now add lots of freshly ground black pepper, the oil, and a dash of cold water. Mix together thoroughly. Taste and adjust the seasoning as necessary.

After 7 to 10 minutes of grilling, put the lobsters directly in contact with the hot coals for a further 2 to 3 minutes immediately before serving. Serve hot with your fresh *sauce chien*.

SERVES 4 AS A MAIN DISH

My friend Madame Rosanne told me that you need to use lots of lime juice in the preparation of the *sauce chien*, because some people are allergic to seafood, and she believes that eating seafood with lime juice cuts down on its allergic properties. I don't know how true this is, but I do know that some old wives' tales have practical reasons behind them.

Matété Antillean
ANTILLEAN CRAB PILAF

M*atété* is a tasty, aromatic crab risotto unique to the French Antilles. It originated from Marie Galante, a little island with a colorful history just south of Guadeloupe. Marie Galante has enjoyed a number of nicknames: *Île d'Ainchi* or *Haitch*; "island of greens"; "island of the hundred windmills"; *Aulinagen,* which means "land of cotton"; *Marie Galante sombrero,* because from a distance it looked like a Mexican hat; and its original Amerindian name of *Tulukaera,* which is also the name of the local land crab. It is fitting, therefore, that the exotic *matété* should also come from Marie Galante. The dish is so delicious it is now popularly served all over the French Antilles. (Pictured opposite page 69.)

3 land crabs or other fresh crabs, about 8 ounces (227 g) each

1 lime, quartered

⅓ cup (78 mL) cooking oil

2 tablespoons (30 mL) roucou oil (see page 103), or 1 level teaspoon each saffron powderand paprika in 2 tablespoons cooking oil

1 pound (454 g) salted, smoked ham hock, chopped into bite-sized pieces (optional)

2 scallions (spring onions), cleaned and finely chopped

3 cloves garlic, finely chopped

Kill the crabs by stabbing them just behind the eyes with the point of a sharp kitchen knife. Rub the cut lime over the crabs to thoroughly clean them. Rinse the crabs under cold running water. Remove the claws and set aside. Now remove the shells from the body of the crabs and set them aside. Cut each of the bodies in half so that each half has legs attached. Set body parts aside. Using your fingers separate and discard the digestive bags from each crab shell, and set aside the crab shells with any of their remaining juices.

To assemble the *matété,* in a large Dutch oven or heavy-bottomed saucepan, heat the oil over a medium heat, and add the roucou oil. Lightly fry the smoked ham hock for about 5 minutes, just to quickly seal and color the outside. Remove the meat and set aside. To the remaining hot oil, add the scallions, garlic, the claws, and the crab bodies. Scoop the contents of each shell, including crab juices, into the saucepan (this is what permeates the dish with that wonderful crab taste).

2 sprigs parsley, finely
    chopped
3 cups (57 g) celery
    leaves, finely chopped
3 cups (710 mL) water, or
    fish or vegetable stock
4 sprigs thyme
1 whole fresh Scotch
    bonnet chile (chilli)
2 bay leaves
Salt and freshly ground
    pepper to taste
1½ pounds (680 g) rice

Discard the crab shells and add the parsley, celery leaves, water, thyme, chile, bay leaves, and the fried smoked ham hock. Stir the mixture, taking care not to crush the chile. Taste and adjust the seasoning with salt and pepper. Bring to a boil and add the rice. Stir again to mix. Lower the heat and cover. Simmer slowly until the rice is soft and cooked and all the liquid is absorbed, about 20 minutes. Remove the chile.

To serve, arrange the *matété* on a large serving platter, taking care to display some crab throughout. Serve hot…the aroma alone will drive you nuts!

SERVES 4 TO 6 AS A MAIN DISH

Court Bouillon de Poisson
BAKED FISH WITH CITRUS COURT BOUILLON

Whenever I think of court bouillon, I think about Yolande Coulls-Lartique. Yolande comes from Dominica but now lives in Jamaica. She writes expertly on Creole cuisine, and we met in Guadeloupe because of our mutual love of Creole food. We enjoyed each other's company immensely and spent hours discussing many aspects of the cuisine and eventually ended up in Madame Rosanne's kitchen so that Yolande could show me her court bouillon. Madame Rosanne had her version too. Now, with a bit of experimentation, I have created my own court bouillon, too, using fresh-squeezed citrus juice instead of wine or vinegar. Here's to Yolande, Madame Rosanne, and all court bouillon lovers around the world. Serve hot with rice, greens, a salad, or cooked root vegetables.

1 three-pound (1.4 kg) whole snapper, cleaned and scaled
4 limes
6 cloves garlic, crushed
1 teaspoon white granulated sugar
2 ripe, juicy oranges
4 sprigs thyme
1 onion, thinly sliced
3 scallions (spring onions), coarsely chopped
Celery leaves from 6 celery stalks, coarsely chopped
1 sprig fennel, finely chopped
2 Scotch bonnet chiles (chillies), 1 green and 1 red or yellow, seeded and cut into rings
Salt and freshly ground black pepper

Scrub the fish, including under the gills, with a quartered lime. Drain, and place the fish in a large, deep baking dish. Rub over the inside and outside of the fish with the crushed garlic, then carefully pour 2 cups (473 mL) water around the fish.

Squeeze over the juice of the remaining 3 limes, then add the sugar and the juice from the oranges. Remove the leaves from thyme stalks and place the leaves on top of the fish. Top with the onion, scallions, celery leaves, sprig of fennel, and chile rings. Add salt and pepper to taste.

Using your hands, stir the seasoning mix around the fish and rub it all over it. Cover the fish with a dishtowel and let it stand for 2 to 4 hours in the refrigerator.

Preheat the oven to 400°F (200°C/gas mark 6).

After marinating, strain off half the liquid making sure that you don't lose any of the herbs in the marinade. Save this liquid. Replace the fish in the center of the baking dish and pour over the reserved marinade. Cover with aluminum foil and bake for about 30 to 40 minutes, or until fish is tender and cooked. Serve hot.

SERVES 4

Gateau avec Citron et Mango

LEMON AND MANGO NO-BAKE CAKE

This is a light, fluffy dessert (very much like a chiffon or soufflé) that cleanses your palate—just the thing after a heavy meal. The tangy lemon flavor remains behind forever.

CRUST

8 ounces (227 g) graham crackers (digestive biscuits) or plain sweet cookies
½ cup (113 g) butter, melted
½ teaspoon allspice
1 teaspoon ground cinnamon

FILLING

2 large eggs, separated
8 ounces (227 g) mango flesh, fresh, or from can, drained
½ cup (118 mL) freshly squeezed lemon juice (from about 2 large lemons)
1 ounce (28 g) gelatin powder
Zest of 2 lemons
½ cup (113 g) superfine (caster) sugar
1 cup (237 mL) whipping cream

GARNISH

4 pieces candied angelica
2 lemons, sliced into thin rings

To make the crust, first grease the inside of an 8-inch (20 cm) springform cake pan. Finely crush the graham crackers into crumbs in a food processor. Alternatively, crush them between two large sheets of waxed (greaseproof) paper that have in turn been placed between clean dishtowels on a flat surface. Use a rolling pin to crush the graham crackers.

In a bowl, combine the finely crushed graham crackers with the melted butter, allspice, and cinnamon. Mix well together and press evenly into the base and against the insides of the springform pan to form a firm crust base. Place in the refrigerator while you make the lemon filling.

To make the filling, lightly beat the two egg yolks, then place the mango in a food processor or blender and blend the mango flesh until smooth. Combine the beaten egg and mango pulp with the lemon juice, gelatin, lemon zest, and the sugar in a double boiler over a medium heat. Pour boiling water into the bottom saucepan. Stir the filling mixture in the top saucepan until the gelatin and sugar have dissolved. The mixture will start to thicken a little. Remove from the heat when it thickens and leave it to cool down.

Meanwhile, whip the cream until it forms soft peaks, and set aside. In a separate bowl, whip the whites of the eggs until they form soft peaks. Fold the egg whites into the mango and lemon mixture, then fold in the cream. Mix until smoothly combined. Spoon the filling into the chilled crumb base and chill until set.

Serve garnished with the angelica and slices of lemon.

SERVES 4

Cassava and Jam Cakes

I had these cassava cakes in Basse Terre, Guadeloupe, where a whole family has built an industry around these versatile tubers. The sight of a three-year-old boy dexterously wielding a knife to peel and scrape a tuber was a unique experience. He had obviously observed members of his family doing the same thing since his birth, and it was second nature to him. I helped his ten-year-old sister, who was pushing the grated, presoaked, and wrung out cassava fibers through a giant sieve ready to be turned into cassava cakes—of which I got to sample quite a few.

Cassava flour, smooth or coarse, can be purchased at various specialty African, Caribbean, Asian, or Latin American grocers. However, should you choose to make your own in the traditional way, you need to allow 2 to 3 days prior to making the cassava and jam cakes.

3 pounds (1.4 kg) cassava tubers, or 2 pounds (907 g) grated cassava or prepared cassava flour
8 ounces (227 g) coconut jam, or any other sweet jam
½ teaspoon vanilla extract
½ teaspoon almond extract
1 teaspoon allspice

To prepare the cassava flour traditionally, peel off the skin of the cassava tubers. Cut each tuber into two or three pieces. Rinse under cold running water then soak in 3 quarts (2.5 L) water of 1 to 2 hours. Discard the water and rinse the cassava under running water. Using the fine holes of a cheese grater or food processor, grate the cassava very finely. Collect the grated cassava and soak it in 3 quarts (2.5 L) water overnight.

The next day, drain off the water and place the grated cassava into a muslin bag or old pillowcase. Pour water into the opening of the muslin bag or pillowcase to further rinse the cassava. Now squeeze out as much moisture as possible from the cassava with your hands. To extract any final drops of moisture, tie the end of the bag, flatten the contents within the bag, and lay the flattened bag on a dry draining board so that any escaping moisture can run into the sink. Place a heavy object on top of the bag (for example, a Dutch oven filled with water or a couple of large plastic fruit juice bottles filled with water). Leave to stand overnight.

The next day, retrieve your almost desiccated cassava from the bag and break it up into a metal sieve. Use your hand to push small amounts through the sieve until all the cassava has been sieved. There should be no unwanted lumps or debris.

To make the filling, in a bowl, combine the coconut jam, vanilla extract, almond extract, and allspice. Mix thoroughly and set aside.

If using prepared cassava flour, place flour into a suitably large bowl, add 1½ cups (355 mL) cold water, and mix to rehydrate the dry flour.

Heat up a large flat griddle. It is ready for use when a drop of water sizzles into a ball and skates on the surface of the griddle. Using a large spoon, place spoonfuls of the sieved cassava or rehydrated cassava flour onto the hot griddle, spread out, and flatten them with the back of the spoon to resemble fluffy white pancakes. Press the cassava pancakes down onto the griddle, starting from the center and working outwards. Place spoonfuls of the filling on top of each pancake and spread it over but not so that it extends to the edge. Quickly sprinkle more sieved cassava or rehydrated cassava flour to totally cover the filling, smooth the tops with the back of a clean spoon, and turn the pancakes over to cook on the other side. You will need to work fast as the pancakes cook quickly—take care not to let them burn.

When the pancakes are cooked, they will stiffen. Lift them off the griddle and allow them to cool before eating, because the filling will be piping hot!

MAKES APPROXIMATELY 10 TO 12 CAKES

The scientific name for cassava is *Manihot esculenta*, but it also goes by different common names depending on where in the world you come from. It has been referred to as *manioc, mandioca, yuca, tapioca,* and *Brazilian arrowroot.* It is one of the world's staple food crops, widely eaten in Africa, the Caribbean, and South America. Certain varieties of cassava are poisonous, and it is advisable to thoroughly wash the tubers after peeling. Grated cassava should be soaked in water overnight before using.

Brioche avec Goyave
BRIOCHE FILLED WITH GUAVA

I guess it is fair to say that brioche is as French as baguette, so it is only natural to combine the Frenchness of the language of Guadeloupe with its tropical Caribbeanness to come up with an original recipe like guava brioche. It should have that typical "brioche look" of a large dough ball with a smaller dough ball on top.

½ cup (118 mL) milk
2 tablespoons (28 g) superfine (caster) sugar
¼ ounce (7 g) packet of active dry yeast, or 2 teaspoons compressed fresh yeast
2⅔ cups (454 g) all-purpose (plain) flour
½ teaspoon salt
2 eggs, lightly beaten
⅓ cup (85 g) soft butter
1 egg yolk
2 tablespoons (30 mL) milk or light (single) cream

GUAVA FILLING
8 ripe guavas
¼ cup (59 mL) cherry brandy
¼ cup (57 g) superfine (caster) sugar

Warm the milk and then transfer it to a small bowl. Stir 1 teaspoon of the sugar into the warm milk, add the yeast, and stir. Leave in a warm place until the mixture starts to froth, about 10 to 15 minutes. Sift the flour and salt into a large mixing bowl. Make a well in the center and pour in the beaten eggs and the frothy yeast. Using clean hands, mix this to form a dough. Knead this dough for about 2 to 3 minutes.

Gradually add the butter, bit by bit. Your butter should be very soft but not runny. Continue to knead the dough until all the butter has been incorporated, about 7 to 10 minutes.

Form one big ball of the dough and use it to pick up any remaining bits of dough around the bowl. Leave the dough ball in the bowl, cover with a dry dishtowel, and put it in a warm place to rise and double in size. This should take 1 to 2 hours.

Flour a working surface or bread board and slap the dough down on it a few times to knock the dough back by getting the air out of it. This done, fold in the dough, pulling the outside edges in towards the center until it is one big ball again.

Divide the dough into eight to ten portions (depending on the size of brioche preferred). Pinch off small amounts of dough from each individual dough portion, about a quarter of the size of each. Roll these small pieces of dough into balls, and set aside.

1 tablespoon (15 mL) guava liqueur, plus extra for drizzling
1 cup (237 mL) light (single) cream
Pink rose petals, for garnish

BRIOCHE TIPS

• To save you having to beat your butter so that it is soft enough to use, keep the butter out of the refrigerator overnight to soften it.

• Do not knead brioche dough as vigorously as you would knead a normal bread dough. Pick up the dough and just slap it down hard on your work surface two or three times and then fold the edges inward toward the center, pressing all the while with your fingers.

• When the dough is ready to prove (rise), I usually put it in my microwave oven (when it is off) because the temperature in there is constant and it is out of the way and unlikely to be disturbed. I can then set the timer to remind me when it is time to knead the dough again or to take it out.

Grease individual small baking pans. Roll the big dough portions into balls and place them in the greased pans. Now mold the smaller dough balls into slightly flattened rounds. In a small bowl, beat the egg yolk in with the milk. Brush the top of each big dough ball with the beaten egg yolk and milk mixture and carefully place each little dough ball on top of a big dough ball.

Brush the tops of the brioches with the remaining egg yolk and milk mixture. This gives the brioches a sheen.

Keep the brioches somewhere safe and warm for about 20 to 30 minutes, or until they have again risen and doubled in size. Meanwhile, preheat the oven to 400°F (200°C/gas mark 6).

Bake brioches in the oven for about 15 to 20 minutes. Brioches should sound hollow when tapped on top when they are cooked.

Meanwhile, prepare the guava filling. Peel the guavas, cut them in half, and remove the seeds. Cut the flesh up into chunks and place in a bowl with the brandy, ¼ cup sugar, 1 tablespoon guava liqueur, and the cream. Mash and mix into a smooth, jamlike consistency, and set aside.

Remove the brioches from the oven, allow to stand for 2 to 3 minutes, then turn them out of their pans. Cut the tops of the brioches off just below the tops of the large dough balls. Scoop out the soft centers and discard. Add the pieces to the filling, and then spoon small amounts of guava filling into each brioche.

Drizzle 2 teaspoons of guava liqueur onto each filled brioche. Replace the tops, garnish each brioche with pink rose petals strewn around it and serve separately.

MAKES 8 TO 10 BRIOCHES

Ti-punch
GUADELOUPEAN RUM PUNCH

Rum punches are used as aperitifs before just about any meal in Guadeloupe, and *ti-punch,* being a local specialty, reigns supreme. I took to it like a duck to water. You can find cane syrup from shops selling Caribbean and Creole ingredients, or make your own by combining either brown sugar and water, or superfine sugar, water, and a dash of Angostura bitters.

4 teaspoons (20 mL) cane syrup
2 teaspoons lime or lemon juice
Crushed ice
1 cup (237 mL) Guadeloupean rum or other white Caribbean rum
4 slices of lime or lemon, for garnish

In a cocktail mixer, put the cane syrup, lime juice, some of the crushed ice, and finally the rum. Shake well.

To serve, put some crushed ice in 4 short glasses and divide the ti-punch between them. Garnish each glass with a slice of lime or lemon. Cheers!

SERVES 4

JAMAICA

Jamaica was built on a sugar economy. The island is the original home of rum, the sugar cane spirit, distilled by planters and on occasion used to pacify slaves. Sugar from Jamaica was called "liquid gold," and it brought enormous wealth to European plantation owners—in particular to the British planters who lived on the island in lavish mansions furnished with European antiques and finery. None of the wealth spilled over to ease the lives of the slaves—that is, the two million and more Africans shipped to Jamaica alone, who actually farmed the sugar.

Although the coastal areas of Jamaica are heavily populated and full of local and tourist life, the inland and mountainous regions are sparsely populated—except for the Maroons in their village communities at Accompong. The word *Maroon* is thought to be derived from the Spanish word *cimarrón,* which means "untamed" or "wild." Maroons are descendants of escaped slaves and of slaves left behind by the retreating Spanish when the British conquered Jamaica in the mid-seventeenth century. After years of conflicts and war with the British colonists, the Maroons finally struck a peace treaty in the mid-eighteenth century and have been living in their cockpit country ever since—a terrain consisting of clusters of small, round-topped mountains densely covered with trees and lush foliage that made excellent protection for guerrilla fighters and runaway slaves.

The Maroons are one of the main reasons I wanted to visit Jamaica. I wanted to see how much of the Ghanaian languages, legends, traditions, and foods still remained. I was not disappointed: stories of Anansi the spider still lived on here in stories of "brer Anansi." Accompong still had Ghanaian Ashanti words like *abeng* (horn blown on ceremonial occasions), *patu* (owl), *abè* (palm fruit), *dokono, fufu,* and many more. I even saw genetic similarities with faces I knew back home. It was uncanny. So to me, the tastes and smells of Jamaican foods were not all new. I felt at home and readily slipped into gear to become a willing local. It was déjà vu, I was home.

Barbecued Black River Shrimp

Black River shrimp are smaller and sweeter than their counterparts from the sea. They are caught seasonally, boiled in salt water, packed into little plastic bags, and sold to travelers to Kingston or Montego Bay. They are irresistible; serve them hot or cold with a salad for a light meal, or as an appetizer.

Juice from 6 limes
6 tablespoons (89 mL) olive oil
Salt and freshly ground pepper for seasoning
3 pounds (1.4 kg) Black River shrimp or other medium shrimp (prawns), cleaned, peeled, and deveined

Mix together the lime juice, oil, and salt and pepper in a large bowl. Place the shrimp in this marinade, cover, and allow to marinate for 3 to 4 hours.

Prepare the coals in a grill (barbecue). When coals are ready, drain the marinade off the shrimp and reserve the marinade. Thread the shrimp on metal skewers, or wooden skewers that have been soaked in water, and grill the shrimp over the hot coals for about 5 minutes on each side, brushing with the reserved marinade. Serve hot or cold.

Variation: Alternatively, you may place the shrimp together with their marinade in plenty of boiling water until they are cooked and pink, about 5 to 10 minutes.

SERVES 4 AS AN APPETIZER OR SIDE DISH

Ackee and Saltfish

When I went to Jamaica for the second time, I was determined to taste the national dish of ackee and saltfish cooked by a Jamaican chef. Chefs have their own versions of the dish, but I got lucky—I met James Palmer, the excellent chef at the Strawberry Hill Hotel. I still crave the taste sensation of the dish he made me that day. When fresh ackee is unavailable (as it usually is outside the islands), use canned ackee. Remember that the salt cod must be soaked in water overnight. This dish needs to be cooked fast and furiously. Serve it hot with Roasted Breadfruit (page 42) for breakfast—what a way to wake up!

10 ounces (283 g) salt cod
¼ cup (59 mL) olive oil
1 large red (Spanish) onion, peeled and cut into rings
3 cloves garlic, peeled and finely chopped
1 green bell pepper (capsicum), seeded and cut into thin strips
1 or 2 Scotch bonnet chiles (chillies), preferably yellow, seeded and cut into fine strips
2 large ripe tomatoes, blanched, peeled, seeded, and diced
Leaves from 2 sprigs thyme
Flesh from 6 ripe ackee fruits, seeded and blanched, or one 15-ounce (425 g) can of ackee, drained
Salt and freshly ground pepper to taste

Soak the salt cod overnight in lots of cold water. The next day, rinse thoroughly to get rid of most of the salt. Taste a piece of the fish to test for saltiness. If still salty, rinse several times under cold water or soak for a further 1 to 2 hours, then rinse. Remove the bones and flake into small pieces. Set aside.

In a large, deep, heavy-bottomed skillet, heat the oil over a high heat and fry the onion, garlic, bell pepper, and chiles until softened. Add the tomatoes and thyme leaves and toss together for a few seconds. Then add the salt cod and ackee. Stir the mixture well and continue cooking over a high heat for a further 2 to 3 minutes until well blended. Season with salt and pepper to taste, and serve hot.

SERVES 4 AS AN APPETIZER OR SIDE DISH

Ackee, *Blighia sapida*, is named for Captain Bligh of the *Bounty*, who introduced it to the Caribbean from West Africa in the late 1700s. The fruit, which is poisonous when under- or overripe but edible when just ripe, is red and looks rather like a ripe pomegranate on the outside. When cut, the soft flesh inside an ackee fruit is pale yellow with big, shiny black seeds. The seeds are discarded, and the flesh is boiled and drained, ready for use in the recipe. The boiled flesh looks just like scrambled egg. It is very mild tasting on its own and needs to be added to strong flavors such as cod—hence, the popular dish ackee and saltfish.

Curried Coconut Shrimp with Sweet Potato Fries

This is a classic Caribbean dish that incorporates a number of ancestral cuisines. The curry represents the Indian influence, the sweet potato the African influence, and the coconut milk the local Amerindian influence. You can double the quantities of the ingredients for this dish, and serve it as a main course with boiled rice molded into pretty shapes. (Pictured opposite.)

2 sweet potatoes, peeled and cut into long flat ribbons
Oil for deep-frying
Salt and freshly ground pepper for seasoning
¼ cup (59 mL) olive oil
2 pounds (907 g) large shrimp (green prawns), cleaned, peeled, and deveined
2 cloves garlic, finely chopped
1 red bell pepper (capsicum), seeded and finely chopped
1 Scotch bonnet chile (chilli), seeded and finely chopped
1 tablespoon mild curry powder
2 cups (473 mL) coconut milk
1 small bunch cilantro (fresh coriander), leaves only, finely chopped, plus additional leaves for garnish

To make the sweet potato fries, pour oil for deep-frying into a large saucepan and heat it over a medium heat until it is hot but not smoking. Season the sweet potato planks with salt and pepper and deep-fry them in batches until cooked and crisp, about 1 or 2 minutes. Remove from oil with a slotted spoon and drain on paper towels. Keep hot to serve with the shrimp when ready.

To make the shrimp, pour the ¼ cup oil into a heavy-based saucepan or skillet over a medium heat. Toss in the shrimp, garlic, bell pepper, and chile and cook for about 3 or 4 minutes. Add the curry powder. Stir well and cook for a further minute, then add the coconut milk. Season with salt to taste, turn the heat up to high, and continue cooking, stirring constantly, until the sauce is much reduced and thick, about 10 minutes. Stir in the cilantro and remove from heat. Serve immediately with the sweet potato fries, generously garnished with cilantro leaves.

SERVES 4 AS AN APPETIZER

Following pages: Sky Juice (page 98)
Coconut Fruit Cup (122)

Pepperpot Soup

Pepperpot soup is without a doubt one of Jamaica's best-known dishes. It is a combination of a West African dish from Sierra Leone and the local Amerindian *cassareep* cooking sauce used by the Arawaks, the aboriginal inhabitants of Jamaica. These days, *cassareep* is not often used but the present-day pepperpot has lost none of its deliciousness. Chefs have their own versions of pepperpot, depending on the availability of ingredients and personal taste, and this recipe is my version of a memorable pepperpot I ate at the Maroon village of Accompong. (Pictured opposite.)

8 ounces (227 g) taro
8 ounces (227 g) yam
8 ounces (227 g) sweet potato
8 ounces (227 g) salt beef or pig's tail, cut into small chunks (optional)
2 vegetable or chicken stock cubes
2 cups (473 mL) coconut milk
2 scallions (spring onions), cleaned and finely chopped
2 Scotch bonnet chiles (chillies), seeded and finely chopped
1 pound (454 g) smoked mackerel steaks, cut into chunks
¼ bunch green spinach leaves or Swiss chard (silverbeet), cut into strips
Leaves from ½ bunch celery, cut into strips
Salt and freshly ground pepper to taste

Peel the taro, yam, and sweet potato and cut them into uniform chunks.

In a large stockpot, boil the meat (if using) with the stock cubes in about 2 quarts (1.9 L) of water for about 20 minutes, or until the meat is partially softened. If not using meat, bring 2 quarts of water and the stock cubes to a boil. Add the coconut milk, taro, yam, sweet potato, scallions, and chiles. Return to a boil, then lower heat and simmer for about 30 minutes.

Add the fish, spinach, and celery, and continue to simmer until all the ingredients are soft and cooked, about 20 to 30 minutes. While soup is simmering, taste and adjust seasoning with salt and pepper. Serve hot, in warmed bowls.

SERVES 4 TO 6

Stamp and Go
SALTFISH FRITTERS

The beauty of Jamaican food, quite apart from the taste, is the colorful names of some of the dishes. *Stamp and go* is the name given to local saltfish fritters. The name is thought to originate from the early days when travelers on foot would stop en route, quickly buy food, and go. No time to waste, stamp and go is the original "fast food" and should be quite salty. The salt cod must be soaked in water overnight. Serve stamp and go hot as a snack or with a green salad as an appetizer.

10 ounces (283 g) salt cod
1 scallion (spring onion), cleaned and finely chopped
1 tablespoon finely chopped fresh chives
2 cloves garlic, finely chopped
2 or 3 Scotch bonnet chiles (chillies), seeded and finely chopped
1 tomato, blanched, peeled, and finely chopped
2 teaspoons tomato paste
2²/₃ cups (454 g) all-purpose (plain) flour, or an equal mixture of cornmeal and all-purpose flour
1 tablespoon baking powder
1 tablespoon fresh thyme leaves
Salt and freshly ground pepper to taste
Oil for deep-frying

Soak the salt cod overnight in lots of cold water. The next day, rinse thoroughly to get rid of most of the salt. Taste a piece of the fish to test for saltiness. If still salty, rinse several times under cold water or soak for a further 1 to 2 hours, then rinse. Remove the bones and flake into small pieces. Set aside.

In a large bowl, combine the scallion, chives, garlic, chiles, tomato, tomato paste, flour, baking powder, and thyme. Mix together well, then add the salt cod flakes. Mix well, and slowly add enough water to form a sticky dough. Taste and adjust the seasoning by adding salt and pepper.

Place a deep frying pan over a medium heat and pour in oil for deep-frying. Heat the oil until it is hot but not smoking, and deep-fry spoonfuls of the mixture until each piece is cooked and brown all over, about 1 to 2 minutes. Remove from the oil with a slotted spoon and drain on paper towels. Serve hot.

SERVES 4 AS AN APPETIZER

Yellowbird

Songs have been written about yellowbird and drinks of the same name have been mixed. This cold soup is an unusual mix of fruit and vegetables and is as interesting in taste as the island of Jamaica is in culture. It is the stuff romances are made of.

2 quarts (1.9 L) vegetable stock, or half vegetable stock and half coconut milk
1 two-pound (907 g) pumpkin, peeled, seeded, and flesh cut into chunks
6 carrots, peeled, topped and tailed, and cut into chunks
2 yellow Scotch bonnet chiles (chillies), seeded and sliced
2 large mangoes, peeled and flesh removed
Salt and freshly ground pepper to taste
4 to 6 sprigs mint or parsley, for garnish

In a large saucepan over a medium heat, bring the stock or stock mixture to a boil and cook the pumpkin, carrots, and chiles until the vegetables are tender, about 20 to 30 minutes. Remove from heat and cool for about 10 minutes.

When the mixture has cooled, transfer it to a blender and add the mango flesh. Blend the vegetables, stock, and mango. Season with salt and pepper to taste. Allow to cool in the refrigerator and serve cold, garnished with mint.

SERVES 4 TO 6

Avocado and Lobster Salad

This dish looks particularly attractive when scoops of the salad are placed in individual iceberg (crisphead) lettuce leaf cups and garnished with bright flowers.

2 cooked lobsters, edible meat only
2 avocados, peeled and cut into cubes
Juice of 2 limes
1 scallion (spring onion), cleaned and finely chopped
1/2 head of romaine (cos) lettuce, washed and cut into strips
1 tablespoon (15 mL) light olive oil
1 tablespoon (15 mL) white wine vinegar
1 clove garlic, crushed
Lots of freshly ground black pepper
Salt to taste
1 tablespoon chopped fresh thyme leaves
Flowers, for garnish

Cut the lobster meat into short, thick strips. Place the lobster meat and avocado in a large bowl, pour over the lime juice, and let marinate for about 30 minutes. Add the scallion, lettuce, olive oil, vinegar, garlic, pepper, salt, and thyme, and toss gently to coat everything well. Cover and chill in the refrigerator for about an hour before serving. Garnish with flowers.

SERVES 4

Breadfruit and Pumpkin Salad with Parsley Butter

This hearty, satisfying side dish features two of the most common foods in the Caribbean—pumpkin and breadfruit. These staples are usually used to stretch scarce ingredients farther; here they get their own chance to shine. It is best to make the parsley butter the day before it is required.

1 cup (227 g) butter
1 teaspoon garlic salt
3 generous cupped handfuls of chopped parsley
1 teaspoon salt
1 large breadfruit, peeled, heart and core removed, and flesh cut into cubes
1 two-pound (907 g) pumpkin, peeled, seeded, and cubed
Salt and freshly ground pepper to taste
1 tablespoon freshly chopped parsley, for garnish

In a medium bowl, beat the butter until light and creamy. Fold in the garlic salt and chopped parsley. Cover and place the bowl in a freezer until the parsley butter starts to firm up. Once it is firm, scoop the butter onto aluminum foil, arranging it in a thick, straight line so that it resembles a sausage. Roll the parsley butter up in the foil and return it to the freezer to harden, preferably overnight.

In a large saucepan, bring about 2 quarts (1.9 L) of water to a boil and add the salt. Gently lower the breadfruit and pumpkin cubes into the water. Continue to boil until the vegetables are cooked but firm, about 15 to 20 minutes. Drain off the water and transfer the vegetables to a large, warmed casserole dish. Add slices of frozen parsley butter (according to taste) to the hot vegetables. (You can save any remaining parsley butter in the freezer for another occasion.) Toss together gently to coat the vegetables with the parsley butter. Season and serve sprinkled with parsley.

SERVES 4

One Can
ONE-POT VEGETABLE JAMBALAYA

One can is an expression often used by Jamaican Rastafarians to describe a whole main meal cooked in just one container. It is another residual reference to a West African cooking style. Ijava, the lovely Rastafarian man who first introduced me to one-can cooking, also explained that this style of cooking can be a stopgap between when you have money and when you are totally broke. This dish is really a vegetable jambalaya cooked in one big pot, and it has become particularly popular with Rastafarians because it lends itself so beautifully to vegetarianism. The beans need to be soaked overnight. Serve this as a main dish by itself or with a green salad.

10 ounces (283 g) dried beans, such as red kidney beans or black-eyed peas
Salt
1¼ cups (296 mL) coconut milk
1 large onion, finely chopped
1 or 2 scallions (spring onions), cleaned and finely chopped
3 carrots, peeled and diced
10 ounces (283 g) pumpkin, peeled and diced
10 ounces (283 g) white or brown rice
Freshly ground pepper for seasoning
3 sprigs thyme (use leaves only)

Soak the beans in lots of water overnight. The next day, rinse the beans under cold running water and drain. Place the beans in a large saucepan and add enough water to reach 1 inch (2.5 cm) above the beans. Add 1 teaspoon of salt and bring to a boil. Boil, uncovered, until almost tender, about 20 to 30 minutes.

Drain off half the water and save it. Return the saucepan with the remaining beans and water to the stove and add the coconut milk. Add the onion, scallions, carrots, and pumpkin. Stir, adjust the seasoning, and cook over a low to medium heat for about 10 minutes. Add the rice and thyme and stir to mix. Add the saved water, cover, and simmer slowly over a low heat until all the liquid has been absorbed and the rice is cooked, about 20 to 30 minutes. If you use brown rice, allow 40 minutes to 1 hour of cooking time. Take care not to stir this dish too much. Season with salt and pepper to taste and serve hot.

SERVES 4 AS A MAIN DISH

Run Down

FISH AND VEGETABLES IN COCONUT MILK

*R*un down is the Jamaican name for a simple but popular island dish called *oil down* elsewhere in the Caribbean. It consists of "ground provisions" (root vegetables) boiled in coconut milk and highly seasoned with saltfish or salt meat. In this version, I use salt cod, which needs to be soaked in water overnight. This is a very tasty and filling main dish. Serve it with greens of your choice.

10 ounces (283 g) salt cod

10 ounces (283 g) smoked mackerel

2 quarts (1.9 L) coconut milk

1 large onion, finely chopped

3 cloves garlic, finely chopped

3 tomatoes, finely diced

2 Scotch bonnet chiles (chillies), seeded and cut into thin strips

3 sprigs thyme

10 ounces (283 g) semiripe plantains, peeled and cut into big chunks

10 ounces (283 g) taro, peeled and cut into big chunks

10 ounces (283 g) yam, peeled and cut into big chunks

8 ounces (227 g) cassava, peeled, washed, with vein removed and cut into large chunks

Salt and freshly ground pepper to taste

Soak the salt cod overnight in lots of cold water. The next day, rinse thoroughly to get rid of most of the salt. Taste a piece of the fish. If it is still too salty, rinse several times under cold water or soak for a further 1 to 2 hours, then rinse. Cut into thick chunks, taking care to remove all the bones. Remove the skin from the smoked mackerel, cut into chunks also and remove all the bones.

In a large stockpot, bring the coconut milk to a boil. Add the onion, garlic, tomatoes, chiles, and thyme. Cook for 5 minutes, then add the plantains and root vegetables. Continue to boil over a medium to high heat for about 20 minutes, then add the cod and the mackerel. Stir and season with salt and pepper to taste. Lower the heat to medium low and continue to cook until the vegetables are cooked and the sauce has thickened. Serve hot.

SERVES 4 TO 6 AS A MAIN DISH

Goat Curry

Goat curry is a favorite dish in Jamaica, particularly at times of celebration. Goats are thought to have been brought to the islands by Spanish explorers, who on their arrival in the Caribbean found little that they believed they could eat or hunt. On subsequent journeys, they brought goats and released them into the wilds of the Caribbean islands. With the much-later arrival of indentured labor from India, goat curry was born. It is best to marinate the goat's meat overnight. Serve this dish hot with boiled white rice, fried plantains, and chutney of your choice.

2 pounds (907 g) lean boneless goat's meat

2 Scotch bonnet or other hot chiles (chillies), cleaned and finely chopped, with seeds

3 or 4 tablespoons (44 to 57 g) curry powder

2 cloves garlic, finely chopped

2 scallions (spring onions), peeled and finely chopped

1 heaped tablespoon cornstarch (cornflour)

2 tablespoons (30 mL) vegetable oil

Salt for seasoning

1/4 cup (59 mL) corn or olive oil

2 tablespoons (28 g) ghee (clarified butter)

2 large onions, finely chopped

4 large tomatoes, blanched, peeled, and diced

1 quart (946 mL) water

Freshly ground pepper for seasoning

Dice the goat's meat. Put it into a large bowl and stir in the chiles, curry powder, garlic, scallions, cornstarch, vegetable oil, and salt. Mix well to ensure the meat is coated. Leave to marinate for 3 to 4 hours, or, preferably, well-sealed in a container in the refrigerator overnight.

In a large frying pan or skillet (preferably nonstick), heat the corn oil and ghee over a medium heat. Remove the meat from the marinade, reserving the marinade. Cook the meat in the oil to quickly seal and brown it on the outside. Add the onions and fry for a further 3 to 4 minutes. Add the tomatoes, the marinade, and the water, and bring to a boil, and season with salt and pepper to taste. Lower the heat and simmer slowly until the meat is tender and the sauce has reduced to a creamy, runny consistency, about 1 to 1 1/2 hours. Serve hot.

SERVES 4 AS A MAIN DISH

Dokono

CORNMEAL DUMPLINGS
COOKED IN BANANA LEAVES

Now here is a true African name and recipe that has acquired a new Caribbean identity. The word *dokono* comes from the Fanti tribe of southwestern Ghana: it is the Fanti regional name for the popular national dish of *kenkey*, which is a boiled, savory cornmeal dumpling eaten with tomato, chile (chilli) *sambal,* and fish. The Fanti version, *dokono*, is usually square-shaped and wrapped in banana leaves, while the equally popular round, southern version called *kenkey* is boiled in corn leaves and sold everywhere. This Jamaican version is sweet, and apart from its wrapping and the use of cornmeal, has very little to do with the original in terms of taste and presentation.

1¹/₃ cup (227 g) cornmeal

¹/₂ cup plus 3 tablespoons (156 g) superfine (caster) sugar

1 teaspoon allspice

1 teaspoon ground cinnamon

4 ounces (113 g) currants

1 teaspoon vanilla extract

3 to 4 cups (710 to 946 mL) coconut milk (or half coconut milk and half ordinary milk)

Banana leaves and string for tying

In a large bowl, mix together the cornmeal and sugar, and stir in the allspice, cinnamon, currants, and vanilla extract. Make a well in the center of the mixture and slowly stir in the coconut milk until the consistency of the cornmeal mixture is thickened but still runny.

Cut 15 to 20 lengths of banana leaf, approximately 10 inches (25 cm) long by 7 inches (18 cm) wide. Bring 2 quarts (1.9 L) of water to a boil in a large saucepan. Immerse half of the banana leaves in the boiling water for about 3 to 4 minutes to soften them. Remove leaves one at a time, rinse to cool them enough to handle, drain, and scoop generous tablespoonfuls of the cornmeal mixture onto each piece of leaf. Wrap firmly and tie the parcels horizontally and vertically, securing each tie with a knot. Repeat the whole exercise with the remaining banana leaves.

Lower the parcels into a large pot of boiling water. Boil, uncovered, for about 50 to 60 minutes, making sure that there is enough boiling water for the full cooking period, adding more water if necessary.

Using a long-handled slotted spoon, remove the parcels from the water, drain, and cool. Peel and serve the contents hot or warm as a side dish or snack.

MAKES 15 TO 20 DOKONO

Sweet Potato and Pumpkin Pudding

This is a typically African-influenced Jamaican dessert. Puddings, like their relatives, pones, are well loved on the island. And sweet potatoes are a traditional food of Africans in the Caribbean.

1 pound (454 g) sweet potato, peeled and very finely grated to a pulp

1 pound (454 g) pumpkin, peeled and very finely grated to a pulp

2 teaspoons grated gingerroot

½ teaspoon grated nutmeg

½ teaspoon ground cinnamon

1 teaspoon vanilla extract

4 ounces (113 g) chopped dried fruits, raisins, or currants (optional)

1 cup (237 mL) coconut milk

7 tablespoons (113 g) brown sugar

1 tablespoon (14 g) butter, melted

Heavy (double) cream, for topping (optional)

Preheat the oven to 400°F (200°C/gas mark 6).

In a large bowl, mix together the sweet potato, pumpkin, ginger, nutmeg, cinnamon, vanilla extract, and dried fruits (if using).

In another bowl, combine the coconut milk, sugar, and butter and then pour this mixture into the sweet potato mixture. Stir well to mix. Grease an 8- to 10-inch (20- to 25-cm) square baking dish or a loaf tin. Pour the mixture into the dish and bake in the middle shelf of the oven for about 45 minutes to 1½ to 2 hours, or until cooked. Pudding should be flat, sticky, and dark.

To serve, remove from the oven and let it stand for 10 to 15 minutes before serving. Serve with cream for topping if you like.

SERVES 4 TO 6

Pineapple and Orange Sorbet

There is something absolutely magical about naturally ripened pineapple—it tastes so sweet! Everywhere I went in Jamaica, I was guaranteed the sweet delight in one form or another; it even featured in designs on linen and bedspreads.

6 large, ripe oranges
1 small, very ripe
    pineapple
Juice from 1 ripe lime
2 cups (454 g) superfine
    (caster) sugar
2 teaspoons finely grated
    orange zest
1/4 teaspoon vanilla
    extract

Cut the tops off all the oranges about a quarter of the way down. Scoop out the flesh from inside the fruits and the cut-off lids, taking care to retain their shapes so they can be used as the sorbet molds. Put the orange pulp into a bowl, discarding the pips, then transfer the pulp to a blender. Place the empty orange cases and lids in the freezer to chill.

Peel the pineapple, then remove the core and discard. Dice the pineapple flesh and add it to the orange pulp in the blender. Blend together. As you are blending, add the sugar, orange zest, and the vanilla extract. Blend thoroughly. Pour the mixture into a big container and then strain it through a medium-coarse strainer (the holes must not be too fine nor too big) to separate the pulp from the juice.

Pour the collected juice into an ice cream container and chill in the freezer for about 2 to 3 hours. When the sorbet starts to ice up and freeze, remove the container from the freezer, scrape the sorbet with a fork or scraper to loosen it up, and scoop the sorbet into the individual chilled orange cases. Half cover the fruit cases with the lids and return them to the freezer until completely frozen. Serve by itself or with fresh fruit of your choice.

SERVES 6

Pineapple and Rum Flambé

This is a visually spectacular dish to make—and very easy. It's always fun to prepare this in front of people when you can.

1 small, very ripe pineapple

¼ to ⅓ cup (59 to 78 mL) Jamaican rum, according to taste, plus additional for serving (optional)

3 tablespoons (23 g) confectioners' (icing) sugar

Heavy (double) cream, for serving (optional)

Peel the pineapple, then remove the core and discard. Cut the pineapple flesh into thick triangles and arrange them neatly in a big frying pan or skillet (preferably nonstick) and warm over medium heat.

When the fruit is reasonably hot, and the juices greatly reduced, about 5 minutes, pour the rum over the top, stand well back and ignite it with a match. Hold the handle of the pan and gently shake the pan over the heat until the alcohol flames have died down.

Sprinkle with the confectioners' sugar and serve with cream poured over, or with more warm rum heated in the same skillet as the fruit.

SERVES 4

Fresh Mango Porcupines

I love to make these funny little "animals"—when you slice the mangoes for the porcupines, there is some fruit left over that you get to eat right then and there! Remember to remove the cloves from the porcupines before you eat them; these spines are for effect only. Also, it is best if the mango is chilled overnight before use.

4 large ripe mangoes
1 box or packet of whole cloves
1 heaped tablespoon confectioners' (icing) sugar

Wash the mangoes and refrigerate them overnight. The next day, stand each mango up vertically on its fatter end and, using a sharp knife, carefully slice off very thick portions from top to bottom on either side of the center stone. Discard the stone, reserving the remaining flesh for another use (or just eat it).

To make crisscross mango porcupines, one at a time, pick up and cup in the palm of your hand the fleshy mango portions you have cut off. Using a small, pointy knife, carefully score a line straight down the middle of the fruit, taking care to cut only down to the outer skin and not right through it.

Allow ¾ inch (2 cm) on either side of the center line and cut another line on each side. Turn the mango portion around and cut the same way again, crisscrossing the other lines. When you finish, invert the crisscrossed mango or turn it inside out so that the fruit bits stick up in the air.

Now place a few cloves (pointed end down) into the mango sections so it resembles a porcupine or echidna. Sprinkle with the confectioners' sugar and serve immediately or return to the refrigerator to chill for a further 10 to 20 minutes and serve cold.

MAKES 8 PORCUPINES; SERVES 4 AS A DESSERT

Sky Juice

What a great name for a plain drink! Sky juice is basically fruit syrup poured over shavings of ice, and it is best enjoyed sucked through a straw. You can buy sky juice in plastic bags from street hawkers in Jamaica. The brighter the color of the syrup, the more popular it is to both customers and bees. Plastic sandwich bags will work for your sky juice, and the quantity of syrup used will vary according to individual preference. Bottled fruit syrups can be purchased at supermarkets. Any combination of syrups can be used; only your imagination limits your choices. (Pictured between pages 84 and 85.)

¼ cup (59 mL) fresh fruit syrup (such as orange, lime, cherry, strawberry, raspberry, pineapple, tamarind, or mango), or more according to taste
Lots of finely shaved ice
Medium-sized plastic bags or glasses

Fill up plastic bags or parfait glasses with shaved ice and pour the syrup of your choice liberally over the top. Insert a straw and serve immediately.

SERVES 4

JAMAICAN RIDDLE

Q: Riddle me this, riddle me that
Sweet water standing
What am I?

A: Sugar cane

Jamaican Jig
MANGO AND RUM COCKTAIL

Jamaican jig is the name I coined for a drink that a Jamaican waiter concocted for me one hot afternoon—after I drank it, I danced for ages. It is made out of mango, the "king of fruits," Triple Sec, rum, water, and lots of ice. In his *Taste of the Tropics,* Mogens Bay Esbensen quotes a rather poetic Jamaican description of a mango as "…a delicious, nourishing breast-shaped delicacy that grown men can nibble in public." I just say that the Jamaican jig drink is yet another polite way to enjoy mango in public, whether you are male or female!

4 large mangoes, peeled, flesh removed and saved
$^1/_3$ cup (78 mL) Triple Sec
1 cup (237 mL) dark Caribbean rum
2 cups (473 mL) ice cold water
Lots of crushed ice

Put the mango pulp, Triple Sec, rum, and water in a blender and blend together for a few seconds until well blended. Put crushed ice into four chilled glasses and pour the mixture over the ice. Serve immediately.

SERVES 4

Coconut Milkshake

Talk about refreshing! This creamy shake is pure heaven—it practically cries out for a flower or little umbrella to top off each tall, frosty glass. You can omit the ice cubes if you like.

2 cups (473 mL) vanilla ice cream
2 cups (473 mL) coconut milk, chilled
1 cup (237 mL) milk, chilled
A pinch of freshly grated nutmeg
Ice cubes

Combine all the ingredients except the ice cubes in a blender, and liquidize. Place the ice cubes in tall, chilled glasses and fill the glasses with coconut milkshake. Serve immediately.

SERVES 2 TO 4

Yeah, Man
JAMAICAN MILKSHAKE

There is no milk in this milkshake, just a fine Jamaican kick from the rum and the coconut liqueur. Yeah, man.

1 cup (237 mL) white Caribbean rum, such as Appleton
2 tablespoons (30 mL) coconut liqueur
1 teaspoon angostura bitters
1 cup (237 mL) club soda (soda water)
Crushed ice
Fruit or flowers, for garnish (optional)

Combine all the ingredients, except for the crushed ice, in a blender. Blend together on low until well mixed. Pour over lots of crushed ice in tall, chilled glasses, and garnish with fruit or flowers as you like.

SERVES 2

Jamaican Coffee

The coffee tree is a native of Arabia and Ethiopia. The word *coffee* comes from the Arabic *qahwa,* or "stimulating drink." There are two main species of coffee tree, *Coffea arabica* and *Coffea robusta.* The *robusta* contains two and a half times more caffeine than the *arabica* and yields a more full-bodied, bitter drink. Many coffee connoisseurs, however, consider *arabica* coffee, which is grown high in the Blue Mountains in the eastern part of Jamaica, among other places, as the finest in the world.

1¼ cups (296 mL) hot brewed Jamaican Blue Mountain coffee, or other *arabica* coffee
⅓ cup (57 g) packed brown sugar
¼ cup (59 mL) Tia Maria
⅓ cup (78 mL) dark Jamaican rum
4 tablespoons (59 mL) light (single) cream
Chocolate shavings, for garnish

Place the freshly made coffee in a saucepan over a low heat. Add the brown sugar, Tia Maria, and rum. Stir and heat until well combined and hot, but not boiling.

Remove from the heat, carefully pour the coffee mixture into 2 heatproof glasses until they are three-quarters full. Using the bowl of a spoon with the curved side up, carefully float about 2 tablespoons (30 mL) of cream down the curve of the spoon onto the surface of each coffee. Sprinkle with fine shavings of chocolate and serve.

SERVES 2

TRINIDAD AND TOBAGO

If there is one thing anyone would note about Trinidadians and Tobagonians, it is that they love their food! Who could blame them? The seas teem with fresh fish, the rain forests are green and lush with natural produce: the array of victuals is almost endless, both in its ready availability and its cultural mix—Indian, Spanish, Amerindian, African, Malay, and many, many more.

Trinidad is not like any other Caribbean island. It is the original home of callaloo, not to mention the steel drum and angostura bitters! Recognizing its beauty, the earlier Amerindian settlers called Trinidad *Ieri,* meaning "land of the hummingbird."

Of the two sister islands, Tobago, the smaller island, is the more African. It has retained many traditional ways, right down to the domed mud ovens (which I swear bake the best bread) and the method of pounding boiled root vegetables into a dough called *fufu,* which is served with soup—a typically Ghanaian dish.

Tobago is so picturesque it is often referred to as Robinson Crusoe island, in reference to the Daniel Defoe story about a shipwrecked British seaman cast ashore on a small, idyllic Caribbean island periodically visited by Amerindians, from whom he fortuitously gained a servant he named "Man-Friday." This story also gave way to an analogy made by some historians: that the slave trade came to the islands when the Amerindians of the Caribbean refused to play Man-Friday to the white man's Robinson Crusoe!

Roucou Shrimp in Garlic and Ginger Wine Sauce

Roucou oil is cooking oil heated and infused with ground roucou seeds (which are also known as annatto or achiote seeds). These bright red seeds are native to the Caribbean and were used by the Amerindians for dyeing and decoration. Roucou oil is lighty aromatic and adds a festive orange color to this dish. You can substi-tute regular cooking oil if you cannot find roucou oil or roucou seeds to make your own (see sidebar). The shrimp should be marinated in the oil overnight. (Pictured opposite page 117.)

1 teaspoon salt
1 teaspoon black pepper
1 teaspoon ground
  cinnamon
½ cup (118 mL) roucou oil
12 to 16 large, uncooked
  shrimp (prawns),
  shelled, deveined, and
  butterflied
2 teaspoons cornstarch
  (cornflour)
⅔ cup (159 mL) ginger
  wine
4 cloves garlic, finely
  chopped
2 tablespoons (28 g)
  freshly grated ginger
½ bunch parsley, chopped
4 scallions (spring onions),
  chopped, for garnish

Put the salt, black pepper, and cinnamon into a large bowl and mix together. Pour in the roucou oil, and stir in the shrimp, making sure they are well coated with the oil mixture. Cover and refrigerate for a few hours or overnight.

Lift out the shrimp from the oil using a slotted spoon and set the shrimp aside. Mix the cornstarch with half the ginger wine and set aside.

Heat a wok over high heat and tip the flavored oil into it. Add the garlic and ginger and stir-fry for about 30 seconds. Add the shrimp and cook for a further 5 to 7 minutes, tossing all the time. Add the remaining half of the ginger wine and continue to cook for a further 3 minutes. Add the cornstarch and wine mixture and continue tossing until the mixture thickens and coats the shrimp, about another 3 or 4 minutes. Remove from the heat.

Arrange parsley on four small plates, place 3 or 4 shrimp on each plate, garnish with the scallions, and serve.

SERVES 4 AS AN APPETIZER

TO MAKE ROUCOU OIL

Heat ½ cup (118 mL) cooking oil until hot but not smoking, stir in ¼ cup (57 g) ground roucou seeds, remove from heat, and let steep for an hour or so. Strain, allow oil to cool, and refrigerate the oil in a tightly lidded jar for up to 4 weeks.

Smoked Herring with Coconut Bread

What a hectic but fun day we had, with Janice Walker in one corner busily cooking herrings for breakfast, some women making coconut bread, some making cassava flour, someone else arranging for dancers, and a man cooped up in his tiny, gaudy, wooden hairdressing salon, perched precariously on top of stilts in the garage. The man was creating the hairstyles of the future on his captive clients. We were getting ready to film the Tobago portion of the documentary series *A Taste of the Caribbean* and the cacophony was overwhelming and exciting.

This dish can be very salty because of the herring, so *do not* add any salt during the cooking. And if you are not a great salt lover, soak the herring in cold water for 2 to 3 hours first, then drain and use them as in the recipe.

COCONUT BREAD
- 1½ teaspoons (3.5 g) active dry yeast
- ¼ cup (59 mL) tepid water
- 2⅔ cups (454 g) all-purpose (plain) flour
- ½ teaspoon baking powder
- 1¼ cups (283 g) superfine (caster) sugar
- 1 tablespoon (14 g) butter, softened
- 1¾ cups (414 mL) coconut milk or water (or an equal mixture)
- 4 ounces (113 g) freshly grated coconut, or 3 ounces (85 g) desiccated coconut

To make the coconut bread, dissolve the yeast in the tepid water and let it sit for about 5 minutes. Then mix together the flour, baking powder, and sugar in a bowl. Add the dissolved yeast, butter, coconut milk, and coconut and mix well to form a soft dough. Cover and leave to stand in a warm place in the kitchen until the dough rises, about 1 hour.

Preheat the oven to 400°F (200°C/gas mark 6).

Form the dough into a loaf and transfer it to a large, greased loaf pan. Bake for about 1 hour, or until bread is well browned and pulls away from the sides of the pan. Serve with the smoked herring or by itself.

SMOKED HERRING

2 large smoked herrings

1 tablespoon (15 mL) coconut oil

2 onions, chopped into rings

2 cloves garlic, finely chopped

1 Scotch bonnet chile (chilli), seeded and finely chopped

2 tomatoes, finely diced

Freshly ground black pepper to taste

To make the smoked herring, remove and discard the heads of the herrings. Clean the skin and break the flesh into small pieces, taking care to remove all the bones. Set aside.

Heat the coconut oil in a heavy-bottomed frying pan or skillet, add the onions, garlic, and chile and fry over a medium heat until the onions are golden, about 10 minutes. Add the tomatoes and herring, season with pepper to taste, increase the heat to high, and fry, stirring regularly, until all the liquid has evaporated and fish is fried dry, about 10 minutes.

To serve, cut the coconut bread down the middle to form a pocket and fill this with the herring mixture, or make a sandwich.

Variation: For a light main meal, serve the smoked herring tossed with pasta and lots of chopped fresh basil, instead of with the coconut bread.

SERVES 4

DRIED SMOKED HERRING

In some parts of the world smoked herring is available only in a desiccated form. If this is the case, soak the herring in water overnight to soften it as well as to rid it of excess salt. Discard the water in the morning, squeeze out excess water from the herring, and use it in the recipe.

Salt Beef Pilaf

This dish is another example of the cosmopolitan nature of Trinidadian cuisine. This time the major influence is Indian, with a touch of soy sauce and nuts to remind you of Chinese and Malay influences, too. This dish can be eaten on its own or as an accompaniment to any meat, fish, or chicken dish. It can even be cooked without the salt beef!

¼ cup (59 mL) corn or vegetable oil

2 tablespoons (28 g) ghee (clarified butter)

½ tablespoon sugar

1 large onion, finely chopped

3 cloves garlic, finely chopped

3 scallions (spring onions), finely chopped

1 Scotch bonnet chile (chilli), seeded and finely chopped

Leaves from 4 celery stalks, chopped

4 celery stalks, finely sliced

1 green bell pepper (capsicum) seeded and finely cubed

3 carrots, peeled and finely diced

2 sprigs thyme

2 cups (473 mL) beef or vegetable stock or water

2 teaspoons turmeric or saffron powder

In a large, heavy-bottomed saucepan heat the oil and ghee together. Add the sugar, and stir until it starts to become golden. Add the onion, garlic, scallions, chile, and celery leaves. Cook for about 30 seconds before adding half each of the celery, bell pepper, and carrots. Add the thyme, stock, turmeric, and salt beef.

12 ounces (340 g) salt
   beef, cut into very
   small pieces
8 ounces (227 g) long-
   grain rice
Salt and freshly ground
   pepper for seasoning
1 ounce (28 g) finely
   ground roasted
   peanuts (groundnuts),
   for garnish (optional)

Simmer over a low heat for about 10 to 15 minutes. Add the rice and the remaining half of the celery, bell pepper, and carrots. Stir and season with salt and pepper. Continue to simmer, covered, over a low heat until all the stock is absorbed and the rice is soft and cooked, about 20 minutes. Should the liquid dry out before the rice is cooked, feel free to add small amounts of extra stock or water. Stir this dish as little as possible during cooking, as the rice will become gluey it if is over-stirred.

Serve hot with other dishes or by itself, garnished with the peanuts.

SERVES 4 AS A SIDE DISH

Callaloo (Tobago)

*C*allaloo is the green leaf of the dasheen plant, whose root is the noble taro. *Callaloo* is also the name of a spicy soup that is cooked with these leaves. There are countless versions of *callaloo*; this one comes from Tobago, from the kitchen of Arlene Kerr. Indeed, each Caribbean island feels passionately about its own *callaloo*; each has its subtle differences. I get the feeling that the wrong word about an island's *callaloo* could easily spark a war!

8 ounces (227 g) salt beef

12 ounces (340 g) okra, washed, topped and tailed, and cut into rounds

1 small bunch dasheen leaves, spinach, or Swiss chard (silver-beet), stalks removed, leaves cleaned, and coarsely chopped

8 ounces (227 g) pumpkin, peeled and cut into chunks

1 onion, finely chopped

3 cloves garlic, finely chopped

1 sprig thyme (use leaves only)

1 tablespoon (14 g) butter

1/2 cup (113 mL) tomato ketchup

1 teaspoon sugar

1 tablespoon ground black pepper

2 quarts (1.9 L) coconut milk

Boil the salt beef in about 1 quart (946 mL) of water to get rid of some of the salt. Drain, cool, and cut into 2 or 3 large pieces. Place the beef and all the remaining ingredients in a large saucepan or pressure cooker and stir together. Bring to a boil, then lower the heat and cook over a low to medium heat, for 30 minutes if using a pressure cooker and about 1 to 1 1/2 hours if using a saucepan, until the meat and vegetables are cooked.

Remove the pieces of salt beef and set them aside. Using a handheld electric beater, whisk the boiled vegetables on medium speed until all the ingredients have broken down into a smooth soup. It is not advisable to blend this soup because blending will render it too smooth and you want to have some texture to it. (Locally, a wooden hand beater called a swizzle stick would be used.)

Break the large pieces of beef up into smaller chunks and return the beef to the soup. Heat the soup through for a minute or two, and serve it hot.

SERVES 4

Callaloo (Trinidad)

*C*allaloo is, as synonymous with the Caribbean as are sun, surf, cricket, and carnival. The eyes of expatriate men and women have been known to glaze over in familiar reminiscence at the mention of the word *callaloo*. I finally understood the look in their eyes when at last I tasted the *callaloo* served by Donna Thomas in the Breakfast Shed in Port of Spain, Trinidad, and the Tobagonian *callaloo* cooked by Arlene Kerr (page 109). Serve *callaloo* hot with Plantain Fried Rice (page 40) or boiled "ground provisions."

1 small bunch dasheen leaves, spinach, or Swiss chard (silverbeet)

8 ounces (227 g) pumpkin

12 ounces (340 g) okra

2 cloves garlic, cut into slivers

3 tablespoons finely chopped fresh parsley

1 whole Scotch bonnet chile (chilli)

Leaves from 5 celery stalks

2 scallions (spring onions), peeled and coarsely chopped

Leaves of 1 sprig thyme

1 tablespoon freshly ground black pepper

2 quarts (1.9 L) coconut milk

1 tablespoon (14 g) butter

Salt to taste

2 teaspoons sugar (optional)

1 pig's tail, cut into pieces (optional)

1 pound (454 g) cooked crabmeat (optional)

Remove the stalks from the dasheen leaves, wash the leaves, and chop them. Peel the pumpkin and cut it into chunks. Wash and top and tail the okra, and cut it into rounds.

Put all the ingredients except the crabmeat into a large pressure cooker or stockpot, and bring to a boil. Lower the heat and simmer, for about 30 to 40 minutes if using a pressure cooker and 1 to 1½ hours if using a stockpot, or until all the vegetables are well cooked and soft.

With a slotted spoon, remove the chile and discard. Remove the pig's tail, if using, and reserve it. Using a hand-held electric beater, beat the soup on medium speed until all the ingredients have broken down into a smooth consistency. It is not advisable to blend this soup because blending will render it too smooth and you want to have some texture to it. (Locally, a wooden hand beater called a swizzle stick would be used.) Return the pig's tail, if using, add the crabmeat, if using, reheat the soup, and serve hot.

SERVES 4

Seasoned Fish Soup with Dumplings

This is a soup that was cooked for me on Las Cuervas Beach in Trinidad. The fish was caught fresh and within the hour Joseph Burnley, my chef, had it seasoned and marinated, ready for the soup. It is all part of the "liming" scene. "Liming" is the local name for hanging loose on the beach and eating whatever is available. Joseph told me he regularly cooks this special soup for fellow limers. I met some wonderful local characters at Las Cuervas, such as Ms. Joyce McLean, who runs the pub on the beach, and many others—too many to list here. I felt honored to be a part of the scene and I wish I could have stayed there all year.

FISH SEASONING
1 bunch fresh thyme (use leaves only)
1 small bunch chives, cleaned and finely chopped
4 cloves garlic, finely chopped
Juice of 1 lemon
2 Scotch bonnet chiles (chillies), seeded and cut into thin slivers
Salt and freshly ground pepper

8 ounces (227 g) smoked mackerel fillets, or fresh mackerel, cleaned, scaled, and cut into steaks
7 quarts (6 L) water
8 ounces (227 g) split peas, rinsed and cleaned
1 teaspoon salt

Put all the ingredients for the fish seasoning in a bowl and toss them together. Put the mackerel steaks into a large bowl and sprinkle over the seasoning and a generous amount of salt. Mix thoroughly by hand to coat all the fish well with the seasoning. Cover and leave to marinate for 2 hours.

Fill a large stockpot with the water. Add the split peas and salt. Bring to a boil and cook, uncovered, for about 20 minutes, then add the plantains, potatoes, and butter. Stir, and continue to boil for a further 20 to 30 minutes. Add the seasoned fish, lower the heat, and simmer gently, covered, while you prepare the dumplings.

2 plantains or green
  bananas, peeled and
  cut into 1³/₄-inch
  (4 cm) lengths
3 potatoes, peeled and
  quartered
¹/₄ cup (57 g) butter

DUMPLINGS
1¹/₂ cups (255 g) all-
  purpose (plain) flour,
  plus 1 tablespoon extra
  for rolling dumplings
Pinch of salt
1 cup (237 mL) coconut
  milk

To make the dumplings, put the flour in a bowl and add the salt. Mix together and make a well in the center of the flour. Pour in the coconut milk and stir to form a dough. Add water as necessary to make the dough soft and malleable, but not sticky. Roll the dough out on a floured board to form long, thick sausages. Cut them into 1-inch (2.5-cm) lengths and add to the fish soup.

Simmer the soup for a further 20 to 30 minutes, before serving hot to as many "limers" as you can find!

SERVES 4 TO 6? 8 TO 10? WHO KNOWS!

Susumber, Fish, and Vegetable Soup

Susumber is also known as *gully bean*. It belongs to the eggplant (aubergine) family and looks like a green pea but tastes like eggplant. Susumber grows in clusters and can taste quite bitter because the beans are said to contain water-soluble toxins, most of which need to be removed through boiling *before* the susumber can be used. Nevertheless, it is absolutely delicious when correctly prepared. The susumber, cod, and shrimp need to be soaked overnight before use.

10 ounces (283 g) susumber, stalks removed, or eggplant (aubergine), peeled and sliced into chunks
8 ounces (227 g) salt cod
4 ounces (113 g) dried shrimp (optional)
2 onions, finely chopped
1 Scotch bonnet or other hot chile (chilli)
4 large tomatoes, blanched, peeled, and pulped
1 tablespoon (14 g) tomato paste
6 cups (1.4 L) vegetable or fish stock or water
1 sprig basil
1 taro, yam, or potato, peeled, rinsed, and cut into small chunks
Salt and freshly ground pepper, to taste

In separate containers, soak the susumber, salt cod, and dried shrimp in lots of cold water overnight. The next day, discard the water and rinse the susumber, cod fish, and shrimp separately in cold running water. Set aside the shrimp in a covered container. In separate saucepans, bring the susumber and cod, in water to cover, to a boil and cook for about 10 to 15 minutes. Drain and discard the water. Allow to cool and shred the cod, making sure you remove all the bones.

In a blender or food processor, blend together the onions, chile, tomatoes, tomato paste, and ½ cup (113 mL) of the stock. Pour the mixture into a large stockpot. Add the susumber, cod, basil, taro, and the rest of the stock. Season with salt and pepper and bring to a boil. Lower the heat and simmer slowly until the taro is soft and cooked, about 30 minutes. Remove from the heat and serve the soup.

SERVES 4

When I saw susumber soup being made in Tobago, I broke down and cried. Only two years earlier, I had been standing in almost identical surroundings in Ghana, my country of birth. I was watching the same elderly aunts who had taught me to cook this dish as a teenager repeat the exercise for my television documentary show. And this time, there I was in Tobago feeling like I was caught in a time warp. The Ghanaian culture has survived and lives on here.

"Ground Provisions" Salad

The term "ground provisions" in the Caribbean is used to describe yams, taro, sweet potatoes, ordinary potatoes, and cassava. "Provisions" implies a supply of eatables and drinkables for survival in time of need, and indeed the term "ground provisions" was coined in the iniquitous slave era, when the ingenious poor managed to devise innovative ways of making the boring but nutritious ground provisions more interesting. You may like to add finely chopped anchovies to this salad, and sprinkle over freshly grated Parmesan.

DRESSING

¼ cup (59 mL) balsamic or other wine vinegar
½ teaspoon celery salt
½ teaspoon mustard powder
Freshly ground black pepper
6 tablespoons (89 mL) olive oil

SALAD

8 ounces (227 g) each of yam, taro, cassava, sweet potato, and potato
8 ounces (227 g) breadfruit
1 large, firm, ripe plantain
½ cup (118 mL) vegetable oil
Salt for seasoning
Half a bunch of dasheen leaves, spinach, or Swiss chard (silverbeet)
Juice of 2 limes or lemons
1 large tomato, sliced thinly, for garnish
1 sprig parsley, finely chopped, for garnish

To make the dressing, pour the vinegar into a large jar, stir in the celery salt and mustard powder until they dissolve, then add the fresh black pepper and, finally, the oil. Cover and shake well until thoroughly blended. Set aside.

Peel and wash the yam, taro, cassava, sweet potato, potato, and breadfruit. Cut into uniform cubes, place in a saucepan full of salted water, and bring to a boil. Boil until cooked but still firm, about 15 to 20 minutes. Remove from the heat and pour the vegetables into a big colander to drain. Hold the colander under a cold tap and run some cold water through the vegetables. Drain, and place the vegetables in a large salad bowl. Cover and leave to cool down.

Peel the plantain and cut it into rounds. In a frying pan, season the oil with salt, then and fry the plantain in batches, turning regularly, until the plantain is cooked and golden brown. Remove from the oil and drain on paper towels.

Cut off and discard all the stalks from the dasheen leaves. Clean the leaves thoroughly in water mixed with the citrus juice. Shake off excess water, dry the leaves with paper towels, and arrange them one on top of another. Roll into a tight sausage, hold firmly, and slice into very fine strips.

Toss the greens in the vinaigrette dressing, then combine them with the root vegetables and mix well together. Garnish with the plantain, tomato, and parsley. Serve cold.

SERVES 4

Spicy Crabs with Cassava Dumplings

This dish is strongly identified with Tobago. It is a local specialty and I can vouch that it is finger-licking luscious. (Pictured between pages 20 and 21.)

3 limes, halved
4 large crabs

SPICY SEASONING
1 tablespoon curry
    powder
2 teaspoons coriander
    powder
2 teaspoons cumin
    powder
1 teaspoon black pepper
1 teaspoon paprika
    (optional)
1 teaspoon allspice
1 tablespoon chopped
    fresh thyme
2 cloves garlic, finely
    chopped
1 large onion, finely
    chopped
1 Scotch bonnet chile,
    seeded and finely
    chopped
$2/3$ cup (159 mL) olive oil

Kill the crabs by stabbing them just behind the eyes with the point of a sharp kitchen knife. Rub the lime halves over each crab to clean. Rinse thoroughly, cut the crabs in half, and using your fingers, separate and discard the digestive bags from each crab shell. Place the crab halves in a large bowl. Mix together the spicy seasoning ingredients in a separate bowl, and then add the seasoning mixture to the bowl with the crabs. Stir to coat each of the crab pieces. Cover and place in the refrigerator to marinate for about 2 to 3 hours.

To make the sauce, heat the roucou oil and the butter together in a large saucepan. Fry the onions, garlic, and chile until the onions are transparent, about 10 minutes. Add the curry powder and coconut milk. Bring to a boil, then add the seasoned crabs. Lower the heat and simmer for about 20 minutes or until the crabs have changed color and their meat is tender. Stir in the ketchup, season with salt and pepper, and cook for a further 5 to 10 minutes.

SAUCE

6 tablespoons (89 mL) roucou oil (see page 105)

6 tablespoons (85 g) butter

2 large onions, finely chopped

2 cloves garlic, finely chopped

2 Scotch bonnet chiles (chillies), seeded and finely chopped

2 tablespoons curry powder

1 quart (946 mL) coconut milk

1 cup (237 mL) tomato ketchup

Salt and freshly ground pepper for seasoning

Sprigs of parsley, for garnish

CASSAVA DUMPLINGS

8 ounces (227 g) finely grated cassava soaked overnight and drained (see page 76)

1¼ cups (170 g) all-purpose (plain) flour

Pinch of salt

Meanwhile, make the cassava dumplings. Mix the cassava, flour, and salt together. Form into small balls about the size of golf balls, then flatten them with the palms of your hands. Bring about 1 quart (946 mL) of water to a boil and add the dumplings. Boil for 10 to 15 minutes, or until cooked. Drain and serve hot with the crabs.

Variation: To make coconut dumplings, substitute finely grated coconut for the cassava and add enough coconut milk to make a firm dough before forming into balls ready for boiling.

SERVES 4 AS A MAIN DISH

Red, Yellow, and Green Salad

These are the colors most prevalent in the Caribbean region. They are found in the natural flora and fauna, clothes, and various flags alike. Serve this salad with hot crusty bread, or as a side dish. (Pictured opposite.)

2 large green bell peppers
   (capsicums)
2 large yellow bell
   peppers (capsicums)
2 large red bell peppers
   (capsicums)
2 large yellow tomatoes,
   washed and sliced
   thinly
2 large, firm red
   tomatoes, washed and
   sliced thinly
1 iceberg (crisphead)
   lettuce, leaves
   separated, cleaned,
   and sliced into strips

VINAIGRETTE

Juice of 1 lime
1/4 cup (59 mL) extra light
   olive oil
1 tablespoon (15 mL)
   wine vinegar or apple
   cider vinegar
Pinch of mustard powder
1/2 teaspoon red paprika
1/2 teaspoon sugar
1/2 bunch basil, cleaned
   and finely sliced
Salt and freshly ground
   pepper for seasoning

Seed the bell peppers and slice them into fine rounds.

In a large salad bowl, arrange the salad starting with the green peppers at the bottom, followed by the tomatoes and the yellow peppers, then the red peppers, then the lettuce.

Combine all the vinaigrette ingredients in a large jar and shake vigorously. Pour over the salad.

Do not toss the salad. Instead, when ready to serve, slice wedges of salad and lift them out of the bowl.

SERVES 4

Cabbage, Carrot, and Cashew Salad

This simple salad is great served with roast chicken, baked fish, or barbecued meats. Or you can make it more exotic by tossing in 8 to 10 ounces (227 to 283 g) cooked, chopped crabmeat and serve it with fresh crusty bread as a light meal.

½ a small fresh cabbage, very finely shredded into strips

4 carrots, peeled and cut into fine strips or shredded

10 ounces (283 g) unsalted cashews

1 cup (237 mL) low-fat mayonnaise

½ cup (113 mL) nonfat milk

Salt and freshly ground pepper for seasoning

In a large salad bowl, combine the cabbage, carrots, and cashews. In a separate bowl or jar, mix together the mayonnaise and milk until smooth, and pour over the salad. Stir well, season with salt and pepper, cover, and allow to stand in the refrigerator for about 30 minutes before you serve.

SERVES 4 AS A SIDE DISH

Opposite: Roucou Shrimp in Garlic and Ginger Wine Sauce (page 103)

Roti with Trinidadian Chicken Curry

Generally, when someone in the Caribbean asks for a *roti,* they mean the whole shebang: *roti* bread filled with one kind of curry or another. *Roti* has become synonymous with tasty Caribbean street food, and many islands have their own version. However, *roti* itself is a tasty Indian flat bread. This is laden with one or more varieties of spicy curry or stew and then rolled up into a bread sausage and served wrapped in waxed (greaseproof) paper. A good forty percent of the Trinidadian population is of Indian ancestry and Indian cuisine has added greatly to the richness and variety of the local diet.

Trinidadian curries rate among the best I've eaten in the Caribbean. To this day, I still smack my lips when I think of late nights in down-town Port of Spain, and the many *roti* breads filled with an assortment of chicken, fish, meat, and vegetable curries that I pigged out on. This dish is perfectly rounded out when served with any combination of boiled rice, greens, green mango pickle, and chutney. Prepare the *roti* and the chicken curry at the same time so they are both finished and hot together, or make the curry first and reheat when the *roti* is hot off the griddle. (Pictured between pages 20 and 21.)

ROTI

- 6 tablespoons (89 mL) warm water
- 1½ teaspoons (3.5 g) active dry yeast
- 1 teaspoon sugar
- 8 ounces (227 g) all-purpose (plain) flour
- 2 teaspoons baking powder
- Pinch of salt
- 2 to 3 tablespoons (30 to 44 mL) cooking oil

Mix together the warm water, yeast, and sugar in a bowl. Sift together the flour, baking powder, and salt into another bowl. Stir to mix and make a well in the center. Add the yeast mixture and enough water to make a smooth, malleable but firm dough. Add more flour as necessary so that the dough is not too sticky or too stiff. Cover the dough with a clean dishtowel and allow to stand for 1 hour so that the dough can rise.

Pinch off golf ball–sized portions of the dough, form it into balls in your hands, and roll the balls out on a floured board into very thin, flat circles. Brush or spray a griddle or frying pan with oil and heat it until hot. Cook the roti one at a time until brown on both sides, for about 1½ to 2 minutes per side. Spray or brush the uncooked side with oil before turning it over for cooking. As you cook the roti, make sure the griddle stays coated with oil.

TRINIDADIAN CHICKEN CURRY

½ a large chicken, skinned, boned, and flesh cubed
Juice of ½ a lime
3 Scotch bonnet chiles (chillies), seeded and finely chopped
2 teaspoons ground cumin
2 teaspoons turmeric, or a few dried saffron strands
2 tablespoons curry powder
2 tablespoons cilantro (fresh coriander) leaves, finely chopped
3 cloves garlic, finely chopped
½ ounce (14 g) ghee (clarified butter)
1 tablespoon (15 mL) roucou oil (see page 103)
2 large onions, finely chopped
4 large tomatoes, blanched, peeled, and coarsely chopped
2 cups (473 mL) chicken or vegetable stock
Salt and freshly ground pepper for seasoning

Flatten each roti with the flat side of a knife or with a spoon to remove excess air bubbles. Keep warm until ready to serve.

Put chicken into a large bowl and squeeze the juice from the halved lime over it. Add the chiles, cumin, turmeric, half the curry powder, the cilantro, and the garlic, and stir well so that each piece of chicken is well coated. Cover and leave to stand in the refrigerator for at least 2 hours.

In a large saucepan, heat the ghee and the roucou oil over a medium heat, and fry the onions until golden brown, about 10 minutes. Then add the remaining curry powder, the tomatoes, and the stock. Season with salt and pepper, reduce the heat to low, and simmer for about 3 to 4 minutes. Add the marinated chicken, stir well, partially cover, and simmer slowly until the chicken is cooked and the sauce has thickened, about 30 to 60 minutes.

To serve, reheat the chicken curry if necessary, and fill the warm rotis with it. Wrap the rotis around the filling and place them seam-side down on a platter or on individual plates.

SERVES 4

Variation: Substitute 2 pounds (907 g) lamb for the chicken (Trinidadian Lamb Curry is pictured between pages 68 and 69.)

Carig and Coucou
SPICY FRIED MACKEREL WITH
COCONUT-CORNMEAL DUMPLING

*C*oucou and fish is a dish about as African in origin as you can get. *Coucou* is made out of corn or maize meal and it can be served with meat or fish, accompanied by sauce or relish. There are many variations of *coucou* in Africa: in Ghana it is called *banku, ugali* in East Africa, and *mealie meal* in South Africa. This particular version has okra added to the cornmeal to make it distinctly Caribbean. I watched Sharon Sullivan and Stephanie Gill in the Breakfast Shed in Trinidad put it together—within seconds, the diners had devoured the lot. Serve this with a green salad. (Carig pictured between pages 68 and 69.)

10 okra pods
1½ cups (355 mL) water, plus extra as needed
1 pound (454 g) cornmeal
1½ to 2 cups (355 to 473 mL) coconut milk
6 tablespoons (85 g) butter
Salt and freshly ground pepper for seasoning
2 tablespoons finely grated ginger
2 tablespoons chopped fresh thyme leaves
4 small chiles (chillies), seeded and chopped, or 2 to 3 teaspoons chile powder
All-purpose (plain) flour to coat the fish
8 mackerel steaks, about 2 pounds (907 g) total weight
½ cup (118 mL) vegetable oil

To make the coucou, top and tail the okra and chop them into thin rounds. Mix the cornmeal with the water to form a thick, runny paste, adding more water as necessary. Set aside. Bring the coconut milk to a boil in a large saucepan and add the butter and the chopped okra. Season with salt and pepper to taste. Carefully add the cornmeal paste to the coconut milk and okra. Lower the heat and stir the mixture with a wooden spoon until it thickens. Stir occasionally until it is cooked, about 10 to 15 minutes. (If you prefer a softer coucou, add small amounts of water to it during the cooking.) The coucou will come away from the sides of the saucepan when it is cooked.

To make the carig, combine the ginger, thyme, chiles, and salt and pepper in a bowl, together with enough flour to evenly coat the fish. Thoroughly coat each mackerel steak with this mixture. Heat the oil in a large, nonstick frying pan and fry each piece of fish on both sides until cooked and brown, about 5 minutes per side. Remove the fish from the pan and drain it on paper towels.

To serve, moisten a small bowl with water. Scoop portions of the coucou into the bowl and press it down, forming four neat rounds. Invert each round over a serving plate, and serve with 2 pieces of fish per plate.

SERVES 4 AS A MAIN DISH

Sweet Bread

Talk about déjà vu! I sat in an outside kitchen in Tobago next to four expert cooks as they prepared several Tobagonian sweet specialties. I felt exactly as though I were ten years old. I was transported back in time and was sitting in an identical situation in Accra at the feet of my aunties Diidi and Chris as they baked their famous cakes and tarts in much the same way—in traditional domed clay ovens, fired with wood and charcoal. Food baked this way has a very special taste and smell. On this day, the sweet bread—really a cross between a bread and a cake—was made by Tobagonian aunties Althea Archie and Margaret. But the best bit was that I was made the official food taster for the day!

8 ounces (227 g) finely shredded, dessicated coconut

2 cups (473 mL) coconut milk

1 teaspoon (2.5 g) grated nutmeg

2 teaspoons (5 g) allspice

2 teaspoons (5 g) baking powder

2 teaspoons (5 g) active dry yeast

12 ounces (340 g) all-purpose flour

½ cup (125 g) packed brown sugar

½ cup (125 g) raisins

½ cup (113 g) butter, softened

Pinch of salt

Preheat the oven to 350°F (180°C)

In a small bowl, place the coconut and ½ cup (118 mL) of the coconut milk and set aside to soak for 30 minutes.

In a large bowl, mix together the nutmeg, allspice, baking powder, flour, brown sugar, raisins and butter. Add the soaked coconut and coconut milk and the remaining 1½ cups of coconut milk and stir into a very soft cake batter.

Grease a large loaf pan and sprinkle with a small amount of flour to evenly coat the inside of the pan. Pour the batter into the pan and bake for approximately 1 to 1½ hours, or until the bread is golden and the sides pull away from the pan. The bread is done when a skewer inserted in the middle of the loaf comes out clean.

MAKES 1 LOAF

Coconut Fruit Cups

Here are three different versions of coconut fruit cup: straight-up, jelled, or creamy and rich—the choice is up to you. (Creamy version pictured between pages 84 and 85.)

1 soursop or custard apple, peeled and seeds removed, and flesh cut into chunks

½ a small ripe papaya, peeled, seeds removed, and cut into chunks

1 large mango, peeled and flesh cut into chunks

1 large banana, peeled and vein removed

4 slices of pineapple

2 ripe guavas, peeled, seeded, and cut into chunks

1 quart (946 mL) coconut milk

1 tablespoon powdered gelatin (optional)

½ cup (118 mL) warm water (optional)

1 cup (237 mL) heavy (double) cream, plus additional to whip for garnish (optional)

½ cup (113 g) superfine (caster) sugar (optional)

Pinch of nutmeg (optional)

Sliced tropical fruits, for garnish

Put all the cut-up fruit into a blender, add the coconut milk, and blend until smooth.

Straight-up version: Chill the blended mixture for up to 2 hours, then serve in tall glasses garnished with fruit slices—or, if the fruits and coconut milk were chilled, you can serve it right away.

Jelled version: Dissolve the gelatin in the warm water and stir it into the blended mixture. Pour into tall glasses and chill for an hour or so to set. Serve garnished with fruit slices.

Creamy version: Add the cream, sugar, and nutmeg to the blended mixture. Whip it all up together in the blender, pour into tall glasses and chill for up to 2 hours before serving, garnished with whipped cream.

SERVES 4

Sorrel, Ginger, and Rum Drink

Sorrel is the sepals of *Hibiscus sabdariffa,* a flower of the hibiscus family. It is widely available dried, and it gives a tang and a bright red color to this drink. Suitable rums to use include Mt. Gay, Bacardi, or Appleton.

1 pound (454 g) fresh sorrel, or 8 ounces (227 g) dried

1 ounce (28 g) fresh ginger, peeled and grated

1 cup (198 g) sugar, or to taste

2 cups (473 mL) rum, or to your preference

Crushed ice

Bring 2 quarts (1.9 L) of water to a boil. Remove from heat and stir in the sorrel and ginger. Cover and allow to stand for 24 hours.

Strain the liquid, then add the sugar and rum, using more or less of either as you wish. Serve over crushed ice.

MAKES 2 QUARTS (1.9 L)

Ginger Beer

Through the ages, ginger has been hailed as a medicinal wonder root. In the Caribbean, Jamaica is this popular plant's main home. Ginger beer is drunk extensively throughout the Caribbean both on festive occasions and more generally. It is also very popular in many parts of Africa. You can use more water than I have called for if you want to make weaker ginger beer.

3 large pieces gingerroot, peeled and very finely grated to a pulp

3 quarts (2.8 L) boiling water

1¹/₂ cups (340 g) superfine (caster) sugar

Juice of 2 limes (optional)

In a large stockpot, combine the grated ginger with the boiling water and sugar. Stir well to mix, then cover and let stand at room temperature (or in a bit of sun) for about 2 days. Strain the ginger beer through clean muslin and store it in a glass drink bottle in the refrigerator until it is ready to drink. Serve cold with ice and stir in small amounts of lime juice if you wish.

MAKES ABOUT 3 QUARTS (2.8 L)

Mauby

Mauby is a light brown, bittersweet drink brewed out of mauby bark. It is a favorite in the eastern Caribbean. The brewing is made easy when you can buy mauby syrup from Caribbean supermarkets and just dilute it with chilled water and ice to serve, but nothing can beat freshly brewed mauby, made from the bark. It is best prepared 24 hours before use.

3 large pieces mauby bark
1 stick cinnamon
¼ teaspoon aniseed
1 bay leaf
1 large piece of fresh
   ginger, peeled and cut
   into four
1 piece dried orange peel
2 cups (454 g) sugar
5 quarts (4.5 L) water
1 teaspoon (2 g) active
   dry yeast

Put the mauby bark, cinnamon, aniseed, bay leaf, ginger, orange peel, and sugar in a very large stockpot. Add half the water, bring to a boil, and boil for about 25 minutes. Remove from the heat and leave to steep and cool down.

When liquid is tepid, strain it through muslin. Stir in the yeast and sugar and add the other half of the water. Stir, cover, and leave overnight. The next day, stir again before you bottle and chill the mauby.

MAKES 5 QUARTS (4.5 L)

Note: Some people prefer to save a little bit (1¼ to 2 cups (296 to 473 mL) of their last bottle of mauby to add to the new mauby, instead of the yeast. Remember, the bitterness is the beauty of mauby, so don't make it too sweet!

GENERAL CARIBBEAN

There are many, many recipes that are common throughout the Caribbean, with each island proudly claiming its own version to be the authentic one. For me, I like knowing that African recipes continue to permeate all strata of Caribbean eating, drinking, and life, and that, to paraphrase the old saying, "You can take the people out of Africa but you can't take Africa out of the people."

So I have put together this chapter of some of my favorite recipes that are not from any particular island—sort of a reminder of some extra-memorable goodies I enjoyed on my travels through the islands.

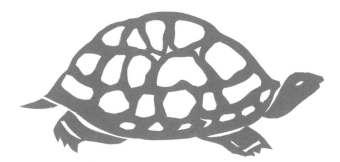

Avocado Mousse

Avocado, scientifically known as *Persea americana,* has many different names; some are quite fun, like *midshipman's butter* or *alligator pear.* Avocados are thought to have originated in Central America, and they were very much in evidence by the time Christopher Columbus arrived in the Caribbean in 1492. Succulent, plump avocados are readily available throughout the Caribbean. They are yet another food credited with medical properties.

1½ cups (355 mL) half water, half dry white wine

1 three-ounce (85 g) sachet lime-flavored or 2 tablespoons (28 g) plain gelatin crystals

3 ounces (85 g) cream cheese or cottage cheese

Juice of 1 lemon

3 ripe avocados, peeled and flesh cubed

Salt and pepper for seasoning

2 egg whites

Assorted salad greens, alfalfa shoots, or tomato slices, for garnish

Pour half the water and wine mixture into a small saucepan and heat over medium heat. When the liquid is hot but not boiling, stir in the lime gelatin crystals. Continue to stir until all the crystals are dissolved. Stir in the other half of the wine and water mixture. Transfer the liquid to a small bowl and place it in the refrigerator for about 20 to 30 minutes. In a food processor, blend the cream cheese, then add the lemon juice, avocado cubes, and some salt and pepper and keep blending until smooth. Now blend in the cold gelatin mix. Transfer the blended mixture to a mixing bowl.

Beat the egg whites until soft peaks form. Fold the egg whites into the avocado mixture. Grease a fluted mold and pour the mixture into it. Chill in the refrigerator until set, about 3 to 4 hours. Serve garnished with the greens, shoots, or tomato.

SERVES 4 TO 6 AS AN APPETIZER OR SIDE DISH

Spicy Plantain and Chicken Satay

If I had my way, everybody would eat plantains regularly. My love of the plantain goes back a long way; grilled plantains served with roasted peanuts (groundnuts) are sold by hawkers on street corners in my native Ghana. This recipe is best served as an appetizer or a light meal, with alfalfa or other green shoots and a tomato salsa. (Pictured opposite page 132.)

MARINADE

6 tablespoons (89 mL) ginger wine
1 tablespoon (15 mL) light soy sauce
2 tablespoons smooth peanut butter
1 tablespoon mild red paprika
Pinch of celery salt

4 boneless chicken breast fillets, cleaned, fat cut off, and cubed
3 semiripe, firm plantains
1 lime, halved
Salt and pepper for seasoning
8 small fresh red chiles (chillies)

Place all the marinade ingredients in a small saucepan and gently warm over a low heat, stirring, until the peanut butter has melted and blended in with the other ingredients. Pour the marinade into a bowl and add the cubed chicken. Stir well so each piece of chicken is well coated with marinade. Allow to stand for about 1 hour.

Peel the plantains, rubbing a little oil onto your hands before starting so that the dark, sticky residue from the plantains' skin does not stain your hands. Rub the lime halves over the peeled plantains so they do not discolor. Trim off the ends and cut each plantain on the diagonal into six thick chunks. Squeeze the remaining lime juice over the plantain pieces, sprinkle with a little salt and pepper, and toss.

Remove the chicken from the marinade, reserving the marinade liquid. Thread alternate pieces of marinated chicken and plantain onto each of 8 wood or metal skewers, and top each skewer with a chile. Brush with the marinade and grill (barbecue) until cooked, about 10 minutes. Take care to keep turning the satays regularly so they are browned and cooked evenly. Serve hot with alfalfa or green shoots and a tomato salsa.

MAKES 8 SATAYS; SERVES 4 AS AN APPETIZER

If you are using bamboo skewers, soak them in warm water for about 1 hour while your chicken is marinating. Wipe the skewers with a paper towel dipped in a little oil before you skewer the meat and vegetables onto them; this helps the cooked food to slide off easily.

Crab Fritters

You can use fresh, frozen, or canned crabmeat to make these tasty morsels. Serve them as an appetizer or with a salad for a light meal.

12 ounces (340 g) fresh or thawed frozen crabmeat, or 2 six-ounce (170 g) cans of crab meat, drained

1 egg

1 cup (57 g) soft bread crumbs

1 tablespoon paprika

2 tablespoons (30 mL) lemon juice

2 tablespoons finely chopped red bell pepper (capsicum)

2 cloves garlic, crushed

3 tablespoons of your favorite chopped fresh herbs, such as cilantro (coriander), lemon-scented thyme, parsley, or chives

2 to 3 tablespoons (30 to 44 mL) olive oil

Salt and freshly ground black pepper for seasoning

Lemon wedges, for garnish

Chives, sliced into long pieces, for garnish

Separate the crabmeat into loose strands using two forks.

In a large bowl, mix together the crabmeat, egg, bread crumbs, paprika, lemon juice, bell pepper, garlic, and chopped herbs. Form the mixture into flat, small patties of about 2 to 3 inches (5 to 8 cm) in diameter. In a frying pan sprayed or wiped with olive oil, fry fritters until cooked and browned on both sides, about 4 minutes per side. Drain on paper towels and serve hot with salt and pepper, garnished with wedges of lemon and long pieces of chive.

SERVES 4 AS AN APPETIZER OR SIDE DISH

Charcoal-Grilled Shrimp with Tamarind

It makes a change to eat shrimp (prawns) with a tart flavor other than the usual citrus juice, and tamarind adds an unusual sour taste that complements the shrimp. Tamarind paste is readily available in various forms in Asian specialty grocery stores. Serve the shrimp with rice, a green salad, and garlic bread.

4¹/₂ pounds (2 kg) large shrimp (green prawns), cleaned, peeled, and deveined
2 tablespoons (30 mL) extra virgin olive oil
1 tablespoon unsweetened tamarind paste
1 tablespoon brown sugar
2 cloves garlic, finely mashed
Freshly ground black pepper for seasoning
2 tablespoons (30 mL) herbed, aromatic oil of your choice, such as garlic, chile, or peanut (groundnut) oil (optional)

Put the shrimp in a large bowl. Mix together the olive oil, tamarind paste, sugar, and garlic in a separate bowl. You may need to add a little bit of water to make the paste slightly runny. Season with pepper. Pour the mixture over the shrimp and toss well to cover all the shrimp with the marinade. Cover and allow to marinate in the refrigerator for about 2 hours.

Thread the marinated shrimp onto skewers and cook on a charcoal grill (barbecue) until they are cooked through yet crisp on the outside, about 7 to 10 minutes per side. You may like to brush the shrimp with a little aromatic oil during the cooking process. Serve shrimp hot.

SERVES 4 AS A MAIN DISH

Rice and Black-eyed Peas with a Difference

A Caribbean staple dish, rice and black-eyed peas lend themselves admirably to experimentation. I have put together this particular dish to remind me of a memorable meal I had in a tiny restaurant in Roseau in Dominica. I am sure it will become one of your favorites too. Soak the black-eyed peas in water overnight before use. Serve this dish hot with any stew, roast, or grilled or barbecued food, or you can enjoy it by itself.

8 ounces (227 g) dried black-eyed peas (beans)
Salt for seasoning
1½ teaspoons baking soda (bicarbonate of soda)
2 teaspoons brown sugar
1 pound (454 g) long-grain jasmine rice
1 cup (237 mL) coconut milk

Soak the black-eyed peas overnight in water to cover. The next day, rinse the peas under cold running water and drain. Place the peas in a big saucepan with about 3 cups (710 mL) of water and the salt and bring to a boil, uncovered. Once the peas start to boil, add ½ teaspoon of baking soda and ½ teaspoon of sugar. Let the peas boil for about 15 to 20 minutes, until they begin to soften but retain their shape. Remove the saucepan from the heat, drain off the cooking water, and save it.

Put the rice in a saucepan or microwave-safe dish, and add the drained black-eyed peas, the reserved cooking water, the coconut milk, the remaining baking soda and sugar, and a pinch of salt.

If cooking in a saucepan, stir well and bring to a boil. Cover, reduce the heat, and cook over a low heat until all the water is absorbed and the rice and peas are cooked and soft, about 20 minutes. If the water is gone before the rice is cooked, add about another ½ cup (237 mL) of water.

If cooking in a microwave, once you have added the baking soda, sugar, and salt to the rice and peas, cover, place the microwave dish in the middle of the microwave oven and cook on High for about 25 minutes.

SERVES 4 AS A SIDE DISH

Sweet Potato and Ginger Soup

This is a very filling soup that can be served hot or cold, although personally I prefer it warm to hot.

3 tablespoons (44 g)
　　butter
1 onion, finely chopped
2 sweet potatoes, peeled
　　and sliced into ¼-inch
　　(6 mm) rounds
1 cup (237 mL) ginger
　　wine
1 cup (237 mL) sweet
　　white wine
4 cups (946 mL) milk
2 teaspoons ground
　　cumin
2 teaspoons very finely
　　grated gingerroot
Salt and freshly ground
　　pepper to taste
1 cup (237 mL) single
　　(light) cream or plain
　　yogurt
A handful of fresh chives

In a large frying pan or skillet, melt the butter and fry the onion until it becomes transparent, about 5 minutes, then add the sweet potato and continue to fry for a further 3 to 5 minutes. Add the ginger wine, white wine, half the milk, the cumin, ginger, and salt and pepper to taste. Cover and bring to a boil, then reduce the heat and cook slowly until the sweet potato is soft and cooked, about 25 to 30 minutes.

In a blender or food processor, blend the mixture in batches, adding the remaining half of the milk. Blend until smooth, pour into a saucepan, and reheat but do not boil the soup. Mix together the cream and the chives. Serve the soup with a small swirl or dollop of cream with chives in the middle. Sprinkle with more chives and serve warm or cold as you prefer.

SERVES 4

Dasheen and Sweet Potato Salad

D asheen leaves and roots (taros) are about as West African as you can get, reinforcing yet again the Caribbean-African culinary connection. You may use either anchovies or strong cheese in this salad; if you use the cheese, then use the salad dressing as well. Serve this salad by itself, as an appetizer, or as an accompaniment to grilled foods.

1 big bunch of dasheen or spinach leaves
Corn oil for deep-frying
1 large sweet potato, peeled and cut into thin ribbons about 3 inches (8 cm) long and 1/2 inch (1 cm) wide
8 small anchovy fillets with their oil, or 8 ounces (227 g) aged Cheddar, pecorino, Emmentaler, or other strong cheese, coarsely grated

SALAD DRESSING
(OPTIONAL)
1 tablespoon (15 mL) corn oil
1/2 teaspoon mustard powder
1/2 teaspoon celery salt
Juice of half a lime

Separate the dasheen leaves and wash each leaf thoroughly. Remove and discard the stalks. Towel-dry the leaves and place five or six leaves at a time on top of each other. Roll the leaves into a tight sausage, then, starting from one end, slice thin strips off the leaf roll. Repeat the exercise with the remaining leaves until all are sliced. Place the dasheen strips in a large salad bowl.

Heat up corn oil for deep-frying in a skillet or frying pan and, when it is hot but not smoking, deep-fry the sweet potato ribbons in small batches, so they brown evenly on all sides. When cooked and brown, remove and drain the sweet potato ribbons on paper towels. Allow to cool down before using.

Drain the oil from the anchovy fillets, and set it aside while you finely chop the fillets. Add the chopped anchovies to the dasheen strips in the salad bowl, add 1 1/2 tablespoons of the anchovy oil and toss together. Sprinkle the sweet potato planks over the salad, toss them into it, and serve.

Or, if you are using cheese instead of anchovies, toss the cheese through the dasheen strips. In a small, screw-top jar, combine the salad dressing ingredients, replace the lid, and shake well for about 30 seconds. Pour the dressing over the salad, toss in the sweet potato chips, and serve.

SERVES 4

Opposite: Spicy Plantain and Chicken Satay (page 127)

Green Mango Salad

Green mangoes are most commonly used to make chutneys to accompany curries, but this salad, made with sliced fresh lettuce leaves and the julienned, semiripe green mangoes lightly marinated in citrus, is simple and refreshing.

4 large semiripe mangoes
3 tablespoons (44 mL) fresh lime juice
3 tablespoons (70 g) brown sugar
2 tablespoons (30 mL) corn oil
1 onion, finely chopped
2 cloves garlic, finely chopped
1 Scotch bonnet chile (chilli), seeded and finely chopped
1 tablespoon (15 mL) light soy sauce
8 ounces (227 g) cooked, shredded, boneless chicken meat (optional)
1 large, whole butter lettuce
2 tablespoons (28 g) crushed roasted peanuts (groundnuts), for garnish

Peel the mangoes, slice off the flesh, and cut it into thin matchsticks. Sprinkle with the lime juice and the sugar. Cover and set aside to marinate for 1 hour.

In a saucepan, heat up the oil and sauté the onion, garlic, and chile for about 3 to 4 minutes. Add the soy sauce and stir in chicken meat (if using). Remove from the heat and set aside to cool. When cooled, mix together with the marinated mango and set aside.

Separate the lettuce leaves and wash thoroughly. Leave four leaves intact and tear the remaining leaves into small pieces. Mix the torn lettuce with the mango and chicken salad.

Arrange a lettuce leaf on each of 4 salad plates and place spoonfuls of the mango salad on them. Sprinkle over the crushed peanuts and serve.

SERVES 4

Opposite: Spiky Snapper (page 135)

Brochettes des Legumes
VEGETABLE KEBABS

Caribbeans eat a lot more raw vegetables than Africans do. Although Africans eat a lot of vegetables as part of their meal (and in some cases, as their only meal), the vegetables are usually well-cooked and are integrated into the main dish. Many of the vegetables in this brochette, such as the corn, taro, sweet potato, plantain, eggplant, and breadfruit are common to both cultures. Serve with grilled meat, fish, or chicken, and a tomato salsa.

2 semiripe plantains, peeled, each cut into 4 pieces
1 eggplant (aubergine) cut into 8 pieces
Juice of 4 lemons
Juice of 1 orange
1 teaspoon brown sugar
½ cup (118 mL) sweet white wine or ginger wine
1 tablespoon (15 mL) corn oil
Pinch of salt
Lots of freshly ground black pepper
¼ of a roasted breadfruit (see page 42), peeled and cut into 8 pieces, or 2 potatoes, cut into 4 pieces
1 taro, parboiled, peeled, and cut into 8 pieces
1 sweet potato, parboiled, peeled, and cut into 8 pieces
2 large corn cobs, husked and with hairs removed, each cut into 4 rounds

Dip the plantain and eggplant pieces into the lemon juice so that they retain their color.

To make the marinade, pour the remainder of the lemon juice and the orange juice into a large screw-top jar. Add the sugar, wine, corn oil, salt, and pepper. Screw the lid on the jar and shake well to blend. Set aside.

Thread the vegetable pieces one at a time onto 8 large metal skewers, adding first a piece of plantain, then eggplant, breadfruit, taro, sweet potato, and finishing with the corn. Repeat with each skewer until all the vegetables are threaded onto the skewers. Using a basting brush, brush the marinade onto the skewered vegetables, taking care that they are all coated well.

Arrange each brochette on a charcoal grill and cook slowly until the vegetables are well done, about 10 minutes. During the cooking, turn the brochettes regularly to ensure even cooking on all sides and continue to baste the vegetables with the marinade. When cooked, slide the vegetables off the skewers and serve hot.

MAKES 8 KEBABS; SERVES 4 AS A SIDE DISH

Spiky Snapper

This is one of my favorite ways of serving this tasty fish in an attention-grabbing presentation. Ask your fishmonger to scale, gut, and clean the snapper. Short blanched almond pieces are readily available in the baking section of most grocery stores. Serve with rice and peas and a salad or lots of your favorite roasted vegetables. (Pictured opposite page 133.)

SEASONING PASTE

1 egg
1 fresh Scotch bonnet or jalapeño chile, halved and seeded
1 tomato, blanched and peeled
1 stalk of celery, with leaves, chopped
1 tablespoon grated gingerroot
1/4 cup (10 g) fresh thyme leaves
3 cloves garlic, coarsely chopped
1 small onion, coarsely chopped
2 tablespoons (30 mL) fresh lime juice
1/2 cup (28 g) soft bread crumbs
Salt and pepper for seasoning
1/4 cup (59 mL) corn or vegetable oil (optional)

1 four-pound (1.8 kg) whole snapper, scaled, gutted, and cleaned
4 ounces (113 g) blanched almonds, cut into short matchsticks
1 bunch greens, washed and dried

Preheat the oven to 400°F (200°C/gas mark 6).

Put all the ingredients for the paste into a food processor and blend on high to form a thick paste.

Place the snapper on a chopping board and use a sharp knife to make three diagonal cuts 1 inch (2.5 cm) apart on both sides of the fish. Fill these cuts with the paste and smear the rest of the paste all over the fish.

Stick the almond pieces upright into the paste so that they stick up in the air like spikes. Also stick almond pieces into the cuts on the side facing uppermost. Grease a large, preferably nonstick, baking pan, place the fish in it, and bake, uncovered, until flesh is tender and flaky, about 40 to 50 minutes. Serve hot in all its spiky splendor on a bed of greens or with your choice of side dishes arrayed around the fish.

SERVES 4 AS A MAIN DISH

Coconut Crème Brûlée

Generally in the Caribbean when people talk of coconut cream they mean the aromatic, creamy white coconut sediment that collects on the top of freshly prepared coconut milk when it is left to stand for a while. This recipe is more a sweet dessert of coconut custard made with coconut milk. The custard needs to be made the day before required.

CUSTARD
1 cup (237 mL) coconut milk
1 vanilla bean
1 cup (237 mL) light (single) cream
3 eggs
¼ cup (57 g) superfine (caster) sugar

CARAMEL TOPPING
6 tablespoons (85 g) brown sugar
3 tablespoons (44 mL) water

Fruit or flowers, for garnish

Preheat the oven to 325°F (165°C/gas mark 3).

Pour the coconut milk into a saucepan and add the vanilla bean. Gently heat over a low heat for about 5 minutes. Do not allow the liquid to boil. When the coconut milk is hot, remove the pan from the heat and set it aside for about 10 minutes, so that the vanilla flavor can permeate the coconut milk, and the coconut milk can also cool down.

Place the cream, eggs, and superfine sugar in a blender and blend until smooth. Remove the vanilla bean from the cooled coconut milk, add the coconut milk to the blender, and blend for 3 to 5 seconds. Pour the mixture into four individual ramekins or one deep 8-inch (20-cm) baking dish.

Stand the dish(es) in a bain-marie and carefully place it in the center of the oven. Bake until the custard is cooked through and firm to the touch, about 30 to 40 minutes if using individual dishes, 1 hour if using one dish. When they are cooked, remove the custards from the oven and allow them to cool to room temperature, then refrigerate overnight.

The next day, remove the custards from the refrigerator. Make the topping by placing the brown sugar and the water in a small saucepan over a medium heat. Bring to a boil and continue to stir until the sugar dissolves and the mixture turns pale golden, about 5 to 7 minutes. Work very quickly to pour small amounts of this caramel over the top of each ramekin of custard or over the top of the one big custard. The caramel syrup will turn hard instantly so you need to work fast.

Remove your crème brûlée(s) to the refrigerator for another 2 to 3 hours before serving. Serve cold, garnished with slices of your favorite fruit or with small flowers.

SERVES 4

Spicy Ginger Cookies

Most people assume hot pepper can only be used in savory dishes but I am here to tell you that chile-heads the world over will disagree with you. I have had chile beer and chile ice cream, and here is a spicy little cookie I made by mistake while trying to recapture a particularly spicy hot-sweet cookie I had in a cafe in Guadeloupe. You know how it is, sometimes the mistake turns out to be better than the original. The amount of chile powder or fresh chiles you use will depend on how hot you like it!

2 eggs

1¹/₃ cups (227 g) all-purpose (plain) flour, plus extra for rolling out dough

³/₄ cup (192 g) packed brown sugar

1 teaspoon baking powder or baking soda (bicarbonate of soda)

¹/₄ teaspoon paprika or hot chile (chilli) powder, or 1 or 2 small fresh chiles, seeded and minced

¹/₄ teaspoon allspice

¹/₄ teaspoon white pepper

¹/₄ teaspoon ground cloves

¹/₄ teaspoon ground cinnamon

¹/₄ cup (59 g) butter, softened

1 teaspoon unpeeled, grated gingerroot

Preheat the oven to 350°F (180°C/gas mark 4).

Grease two nonstick baking sheets. In a cup, beat the eggs with a fork. Sieve the flour, sugar, baking powder, paprika (if using), allspice, white pepper, cloves, and cinnamon together into a large mixing bowl. Mix in the butter, ginger, and chile (if using), then make a well in the center and pour the beaten eggs into the well. Use a wooden spoon to mix together into a soft dough.

Divide the dough into two and roll out one piece on a lightly floured board with a floured rolling pin. Take care to flour your hands too before handling the dough. Roll the dough flat to about ¹/₈-inch (3 mm) thick. Cut the dough into 2-inch (5 cm) squares. The dough will be quite sticky so flour the knife in between cuts and use it to lift up the squares of dough. Arrange them on the baking sheets, leaving a space of about ¹/₂ inch (1 cm) between each square. Repeat the process with the other half of the dough until all the dough is used up.

Alternatively, you may pinch off small portions of dough the size of glass marbles and press them with your floured hands into 2-inch (5-cm) round shapes, instead of rolling the dough and cutting it into squares.

Bake the cookies for about 10 minutes or until golden. Remove the baking sheets from the oven and allow to cool for about 15 minutes before lifting the cookies off the sheet and transferring them to a wire rack to cool completely. Transfer the cool cookies to an airtight container for later use, or serve as you wish.

MAKES ABOUT 36 COOKIES

Soused Mangoes

If you can't beat them, join them—mango joins the ranks of rum drinkers and gets soused!

4 large semiripe mangoes, washed and dried
3 tablespoons (48 g) packed brown sugar
1 cup (237 mL) dark Caribbean rum
¼ cup (59 mL) Triple Sec
Pinch of freshly grated nutmeg
Soursop pulp, for topping (optional)
Heavy (double) cream, for topping (optional)
4 sprigs mint, for garnish (optional)

Cut the mangoes into thin slices, leaving the skin on. In a large dessert bowl, arrange a layer of mango and sprinkle over some sugar. Continue this process until all the mango has been used. Carefully pour the rum and then the Triple Sec all over the slices of mango, and garnish with the grated nutmeg. Cover and place the dish in the refrigerator overnight. Serve chilled with seeded, blended soursop pulp or heavy cream as a topping, or by itself, garnishing each serving with a sprig of mint.

SERVES 4

Piña Colada

A piña colada is the result of the perfect marriage between rum and pine-apple juice, with coconut cream an essential witness. It is designed to quench the most ardent of thirsts over and over again.

4 cups (946 mL) pineapple juice
2 cups (473 mL) white rum
1¼ cups (296 mL) coconut cream
Juice of 2 fresh limes
Lots of crushed ice

Combine all the ingredients in a blender and liquidize. Pour into chilled glasses and serve immediately.

SERVES 4 TO 6

Soursop Milkshake

Soursops are a very popular fruit in the Caribbean. A native of tropical America, they are also known as *guanabana* and are found in many of the islands. The fruit is slightly heart-shaped, big—about 6 to 8 inches (15 to 20 cm) long—and dark green with a spiny surface. Inside, it most closely resembles the custard apple, with its white flesh and black pips. Soursop is almost always eaten raw, but because it retains its flavor well, it is also used to make ice cream, drinks, sherbet, sorbets, and occasionally, soufflés. Sometimes it is just served like cream to accompany other fruits or desserts.

2 ripe soursops, or 2 large ripe custard apples

1 quart (946 mL) lowfat milk

2 teaspoons (10 g) superfine (caster) sugar (optional)

Grated nutmeg, for garnish

Cut open the fruits and scoop the custardlike white flesh into a bowl. Remove all the black pips and combine the remaining flesh with the milk and the sugar (if using) in a blender. Blend on high speed until smooth, about 1 or 2 minutes. Pour the mixture through a sieve into chilled glasses and serve cold, with a little grated nutmeg sprinkled on top as garnish.

SERVES 4

CONVERSION CHARTS

▼ VOLUME

1 teaspoon = 4.93 mL = 5 mL

1 tablespoon = 14.79 mL/3 teaspoons = 15 mL

1 cup = 236.59 mL/16 tablespoons = 250 mL

1 L = 202.88 teaspoons/67.63 tablespoons/4.23 cups = 1 quart/4 cups

IMPERIAL MEASURE	APPROXIMATE METRIC MEASURE	ACTUAL METRIC MEASURE
1 teaspoon	5 mL	5 mL
2 teaspoons	10 mL	10 mL
3 teaspoons (1 tablespoon)	15 mL	15 mL
1$\frac{1}{2}$ tablespoons	22.5 mL	22 mL
2 tablespoons	30 mL	30 mL
3 tablespoons	45 mL	44 mL
4 tablespoons ($\frac{1}{4}$ cup)	60 mL	59 mL
5 tablespoons	75 mL	74 mL
$\frac{1}{3}$ cup	80 mL	78 mL
6 tablespoons	90 mL	89 mL
7 tablespoons	105 mL	104 mL
8 tablespoons ($\frac{1}{2}$ cup)	125 mL	118 mL
9 tablespoons	135 mL	133 mL
10 tablespoons	150 mL	148 mL
$\frac{2}{3}$ cup	160 mL	159 mL
11 tablespoons	165 mL	163 mL
12 tablespoons ($\frac{3}{4}$ cup)	180 mL	177 mL
13 tablespoons	195 mL	192 mL
14 tablespoons	210 mL	207 mL
15 tablespoons	225 mL	222 mL
1 cup	250 mL	237 mL
2 cups	500 mL	473 mL
3 cups	750 mL	710 mL
4 cups (1 quart)	1 L	946 mL
5 cups	1.25 L	1.2 L
6 cups	1.5 L	1.4 L
7 cups	1.75 L	1.7 L
8 cups (2 quarts)	2 L	1.9 L

▼ WEIGHT

1 ounce = 28.35 g = 30 g
1 pound = 453.59 g/16 ounces = 500 g
1 kg = 2.2 pounds = 2 pounds

IMPERIAL MEASURE	APPROXIMATE METRIC MEASURE	ACTUAL METRIC MEASURE
$1/2$ ounce	15 g	14 g
1 ounce	30 g	28 g
$1^1/2$ ounces	45 g	43 g
2 ounces	60 g	57 g
$2^1/2$ ounces	75 g	71 g
3 ounces	90 g	85 g
$3^1/2$ ounces	105 g	100 g
4 ounces ($1/4$ pound)	125 g	113 g
$4^1/2$ ounces	140 g	128 g
5 ounces	155 g	142 g
$5^1/2$ ounces	170 g	156 g
6 ounces	185 g	170 g
$6^1/2$ ounces	200 g	184 g
7 ounces	220 g	198 g
$7^1/2$ ounces	235 g	213 g
8 ounces ($1/2$ pound)	250 g	227 g
$8^1/2$ ounces	265 g	241 g
9 ounces	280 g	255 g
$9^1/2$ ounces	295 g	270 g
10 ounces	310 g	283 g
$10^1/2$ ounces	325 g	298 g
11 ounces	345 g	312 g
$11^1/2$ ounces	360 g	326 g
12 ounces ($3/4$ pound)	375 g	340 g
$12^1/2$ ounces	390 g	354 g
13 ounces	410 g	369 g
$13^1/2$ ounces	425 g	383 g
14 ounces	440 g	397 g
$14^1/2$ ounces	455 g	411 g
15 ounces	470 g	425 g
$15^1/2$ ounces	485 g	439 g
16 ounces (1 pound)	500 g	454 g
$1^1/2$ pounds	750 g	680 g
2 pounds	1 kg	907 g

GLOSSARY

Allspice The berry of *Pimenta dioica.* Used ground to season many Caribbean dishes; if unavailable, an equal mixture of ground nutmeg, cinnamon, and cloves may be used.

Bain-marie A baking pan containing hot water into which another pan filled with food is placed to cook the contents.

Black-eyed peas The seeds of *Vigna sinensis.* Originally from China, now widely used as a staple food in the Caribbean, the southern United States, and Africa. Also known as *black-eyed beans.*

Bouquet garni A selection of aromatic plants tied together in a small bundle, used to flavor a sauce or stock. Bouquets garnis usually consist of two or three sprigs or parsley, a sprig of thyme, and one or two dried bay leaves, but their composition may vary.

Cassava The edible, starchy root of *Manihot esculenta.* A popular staple vegetable. The toxic hydrocyanic acid cassava contains can be eliminated by soaking and/or cooking the flesh. Also known as *manioc, mandioca,* or *yuca.*

Conch *Strombus gigas,* a large gastropod mollusk. The flesh is sweet-tasting, but tough, and needs to be thoroughly tenderized before it is cooked. The meat of another large mollusk, such as abalone, can be used as a substitute. Also known as *lambi* in the French-speaking areas of the Caribbean.

Custard apple The fruit of *Annona cherimola.* Grayish green to black on the outside, with a sweet, refreshing flesh the consistency of custard. Also known as *cherimoya.*

Dasheen The *Colocasia esculenta* plant, especially its edible leaves. See page 108. Also known as *callaloo* and *taro.*

Giambo See **Okra;** on Dutch-speaking Caribbean islands, giambo also refers to a thick and tasty okra soup with shrimp and fish.

Guava The fruit of *Psidium guajava,* a tree native to tropical America. Fruit is round to oval shaped, a yellowish-orange color when ripe. The flesh is pink and full of small, edible seeds. Guavas are eaten raw or stewed and served as a dessert; peeled and eaten fresh out of the hand or in a bowl with cream; added to fruit salads or fruit platters and made into guava jelly.

Okra The edible pods of *Hibiscus esculentus.* Okra pods have a distinctive, slimy texture, and are often added to soups and stews to thicken them. Also known as *okro, ladies' fingers, bamie, bamia, gamya, quimbombo, ochros, bindi, giambo,* and *gumbo* in various parts of the Caribbean.

Papaya A large tropical fruit, *Carica papaya,* with a smooth green skin that turns bright orange-yellow when ripe. Rich in vitamins B and C, papaya can be cooked as a vegetable when unripe or eaten as a fruit when ripe. Papain, the protein-digesting enzyme in green papayas, is used as a meat tenderizer. Also known as *pawpaw, papaye, tree melon, lechosa, fruit of angels,* and *fruta bomba.*

Plantain   The fruits of *Musa paradiciaca,* or *M. sapientum,* members of the banana family. Widely used as a staple food, plantains are bigger, firmer, and starchier than bananas, and need to be cooked before they can be eaten. For instructions on peeling plantains, see page 37.

Roucou   The triangular red seeds of *Bixa orellana,* a shrub native to tropical America, which are ground into an orange-red powder used as a coloring agent in Caribbean foods, including angostura bitters. If unavailable, substitute a combination of paprika and saffron powder mixed with a little oil. To make roucou oil for cooking, see page 103. Also known as *annatto, achiote,* or *woucou.*

Saltfish   Usually, salted codfish or salted mackerel, a prized staple of Caribbean cooking. Should be soaked in water overnight before using.

Soursop   *Annona reticula,* a fruit native to South America. Heart-shaped with a slightly prickly green skin and sweet, whitish flesh the consistency of thick custard. Used in drinks and instead of cream as a topping for desserts. Custard apples (cherimoyas) can be substituted. Also known as *guanabana* or *corossol.*

Sweet potatoes   The edible tuber of *Ipomoea batatas.* Sweet potatoes have orange skin and pale to deep orange flesh; they are often confused with yams, but are not related.

Tamarind   The fruit of *Tamarindus indica.* See page 35.

Taro   The edible tuber of the dasheen, or *Colocasia esculenta* plant. See page 108.

Yam   The round or elongated tuber of *Dioscorea spp.* Yams vary in color from white to purplish, have hairy skins, and can grow to hundreds of pounds in weight! They are used the same way potatoes or sweet potatoes are used.

INDEX

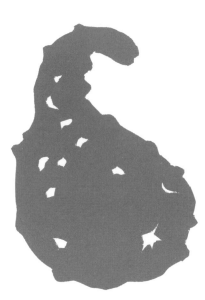